# *Contents*

# HOW TO
## YOUR
## TO
## M

## OMAN

**Bromley**
THE LONDON BOROUGH
www.bromley.gov.uk

Please return/renew this item
by the last date shown.
Books may also be renewed by
phone and Internet.

SQUARFONE
s

**Bromley Libraries**

The information and advice contained in this book are based upon the research and the personal and professional experiences of the authors. They are not intended as a substitute for consulting with a health care professional. The publisher and authors are not responsible for any adverse effects or consequences resulting from the use of any of the suggestions, preparations, or procedures discussed in this book. All matters pertaining to the physical health of you or your child should be supervised by a health care professional. It is advisable to secure more than one opinion in considering any course of treatment or other healthcare related decisions.

Editors: Janet Gauger, Philip Maffetone • Cover Designer: Jeannie Tudor
Typesetter: Gary A. Rosenberg • Cover Photography: Sherman Hines
Photography: Sherman Hines, Jim Kaliss, Jerold Morantz, Kerper Studio, Inc.

**Square One Publishers**
115 Herricks Road • Garden City Park, NY 11040
(516) 535-2010 • (877) 900-BOOK • www.squareonepublishers.com

**Library of Congress Cataloging-in-Publication Data**

Doman, Douglas.
   How to teach your baby to swim / Douglas Doman.
      p. cm.
   Includes index.
   ISBN-13: 978-0-7570-0198-7 (pbk.)
   ISBN-10: 0-7570-0198-X (pbk.)
   ISBN-13: 978-0-7570-0197-0 (hardback)
   ISBN-10: 0-7570-0197-1 (hardback)
   1. Swimming for infants—Study and teaching. 2. Swimmin
I. Title.

GV837.25.D66 2006
797.2'10832—dc22

2006018601

Copyright © 2006 by Douglas Doman.

*The Institutes for the Achievement of Human Potential, The Institutes, Dot Cards, Bit of Intelligence, What To Do About Your Brain-Injured Child, How To Multiply Your Baby's Intelligence, The Gentle Revolution, Better Baby,* and the *"Boy on Hand"* logo are registered trademarks of The Institutes for the Achievement of Human Potential and Registered in the U.S. Patent and Trademark Office.

*How To Teach Your Baby To Read, How To Teach Your Baby Math, How To Give Your Baby Encyclopedic Knowledge, How To Teach Your Baby To Be Physically Superb, How Smart Is Your Baby?, How To Teach Your Baby To Swim, the Developmental Profile,* and *IAHP* are trademarks of The Institutes for the Achievement of Human Potential.

Glenn Doman is a registered trademark and service mark of Glenn Doman (Registered in the U.S. Patent and Trademark Office) and is used with his permission.

Printed in the United States of America

10   9   8   7   6   5   4   3   2   1

*For my mother and father,*
*Katie Massingham Doman*
*and*
*Glenn Joseph Doman,*
*who arranged for me to go through life*
*standing on their shoulders.*

# *Foreword*

A child's level of physical activity is directly related to, and is a vital component of, overall health and fitness. This includes assisting in the development of virtually all systems of the body and establishing a lifetime of various mental and physical benefits. Physical *inactivity* is damaging, and is the start of a long process of injury that can only worsen with age. The decision to be active, and its implementation, is best made early in life, ideally immediately after birth.

Of profound importance is the impact swimming has on a baby's developing brain. This includes not only physical development, but intellectual proficiency as well. The sooner a child is exposed to these great benefits, the sooner and more effectively the brain responds to them. After all, next to eating, the baby's primary task is learning. Babies should be raised *on purpose*, not by accident.

The period to take advantage of this phenomenal development is relatively short, as the child's brain essentially reaches maximum growth by around six years of age.

Newborns can perform very little physical activity, except when in the water. At this age swimming is the best way to pursue a healthy and fit life, including the encouragement of optimal brain growth and development. The only other factor needed is you.

You and your baby will embark on an incredible journey, and this book is a roadmap. The author provides a simple program with a very high level of effectiveness. It's the result of more than fifty years of search and discovery with both brain-injured and well children by the staff of The Institutes for the Achievement of Human Potential. This continuous quest for answers to the problems children face has taken the most senior members of the team around the world—from the Xingu in Brazil Centrale to the Bushman of the Kalahari Desert—and back to mankind's earliest beginnings.

The author literally grew up at The Institutes, founded by his father, Glenn Doman. Glenn's half-century of helping brain-injured children function better through crawling, creeping, walking, swimming, and running, and of helping well children to achieve extraordinary brain function, is discussed in his books *How To Teach Your Baby To Be Physically Superb* and *What To Do About Your Brain-Injured Child*.

I was asked to edit this book because of my extensive experience in working with some of the world's top swimmers and other athletes, and because of my work at The Institutes in the area of brain development.

The program outlined in this book will not only be a great beginning for your child's overall development, but it will help you recover from pregnancy and further strengthen the family bond.

As a mother, perhaps your most important responsibility is to help your child develop into the best human being possible. There is no better time to provide this opportunity than now.

Dr. Philip Maffetone
*Consultant to professional athletes,*
*Past president, The International College*
*of Applied Kinesiology*

# *Introduction*

**B**abies love to swim.

They should have the opportunity to swim right from birth. In fact, swimming helps to stimulate brain growth and development at a critical time. Swimming also provides an excellent opportunity for the newborn baby to develop physically when it is difficult for him to move on land.

It is especially important for the newborn baby to have the opportunity to move in the first few days and weeks of life. When born the baby has the advantage of being light in weight but the disadvantage of being inexperienced in movement. If given the opportunity to move each day, the baby will gain much-needed experience, but will also gain weight.

This makes his job more difficult.

The newborn is in a race against time. The baby must gain mobility function *before* he gains too much weight. Swimming provides an ideal opportunity for the newborn to move in an environment where he will actually be buoyant and where baby fat will be advantageous rather than making life more difficult.

In truth the newborn has actually been "swimming" in utero for months. Swimming is one of the most sophisticated brain functions the baby has at birth.

It is a fact that the brain literally grows by use. Swimming is one of many ways that we can provide sensory stimulation and opportunity that grow the brain. If we are smart about providing appropriate stimulation and opportunity, then teaching the baby will be a joyous process for mother and baby.

It is common for the children we teach at *The Institutes for the*

*Achievement of Human Potential* to be excellent swimmers, but they also excel in running, biking, gymnastics, and ballet by the time they are six years old. The sum of these activities is much greater than each alone.

Since 1977 thousands of mothers have attended The Institutes *How To Multiply Your Baby's Intelligence* course. These mothers returned home to help their babies develop to very high levels of brain function.

Our work with brain-injured and well children has supported what we know to be true—all babies are "water babies." The mission of *The Institutes* is to teach parents how to help their children reach high levels of physical, intellectual, and social ability.

*The Institutes* is a research and teaching organization. It is our responsibility to create new methods to develop the brain of both the brain-injured and well child, and teach those methods to parents. This book is part of that process.

The baby will reap many benefits from learning to swim right from birth. He will develop better physical strength and coordination. These abilities will enhance the ability to crawl on the belly and to creep on hands and knees. Our babies are "floor babies" and they learn how to move against the force of gravity. It is truly a miracle in twelve months that the baby's brain—which had very little information about moving in gravity—has developed intricate sensory and motor areas in such a short period of time.

As a baby develops these mobility functions, breathing will become deeper, more regular, and more mature. This enhanced respiration helps the baby to be able to make sounds, which improves communication and overall language development. When the baby can move better, and breathe better, health also improves. When the baby is able to communicate better with mother and father, baby is happier and more content. These are all valuable "side effects" of learning to swim.

The newborn progresses, becomes more confident, and becomes a true "water baby." The baby learns how to handle himself in the water. Ultimately the baby will be much safer in the water than other children who may be twice the age.

An adventure has begun from the newborn's initial swim to the first walking steps. Along the way the baby will make a thousand mobility experiments to discover what to do and how to do it. Swimming is literally the springboard for this adventure and these discoveries.

The objective of this book is to teach mothers and fathers how to teach their baby not only to swim, but to adore swimming. By so doing, the baby will gain many other abilities that will serve him throughout life.

# 1

---

# *Newborns Can Swim!*

About eight weeks after conception the fetus has limbs that move frequently. Living in the water of the womb, the baby moves in this environment for the next seven months.

Adults sometimes look upon newborns as weak, immobile creatures. On the contrary, newborns are born swimmers. If we allow them to continue to be in water, they will not lose that ability.

Beginning at around four months of fetal life, mother often feels her unborn baby kick as he moves his arms and legs. As the baby grows and develops, the movements become stronger and eventually become so powerful they can wake mother during the night.

After months of floating in utero, newborns are capable of continuing their natural swimming ability. Their first purposeful movements may come in the water, the topic of this chapter. Only afterwards do they learn to crawl, the initial step that leads to creeping, walking, and running.

Arnold Gessel, one of the great child developmentalists, said that the floor is the athletic field of the child. At The Institutes for the Achievement of Human Potential, all of our mothers give their babies unlimited opportunity to be on the floor to move. Our babies are "floor babies." The companion book to this one, *How To Teach Your Baby To Be Physically Superb*, teaches parents everything they need to know about developing their babies' mobility from birth to age six.

Our babies are also "water babies." From the first day of life they are given the opportunity to be in the water and swim.

Our philosophy is *The magic is in the child*. When it comes to mobility, we give babies opportunity and allow nature to take its course. When newborns are given the opportunity to be in water, they relax and enjoy the freedom of movement.

At birth the baby's brain has little information about how to move on the floor because he has never had that experience. However, the baby already has seven months of information about how it feels to move in an aqueous environment. In this environment the neonate's body is buoyant. All the baby's sensory pathways are developing—vision, hearing, feeling, taste, and smell sensation. Motor pathways are also programmed by physical movement.

If newborns don't use their natural ability, it may be lost. For this reason it is very important that they have the opportunity to swim from the very first day of life or as soon as possible. *Learning how to swim is an inverse function of age.* It is easier to teach a five-year-old to swim than a six-year-old, a three-year-old than a four-year-old, and a one-year-old than a two-year-old. Newborn babies already know how to swim, so we really don't need to teach them much. We only need to give them the opportunity to use what they have learned in utero.

Perhaps the best news of all is that swimming helps to grow and develop the baby's brain, because the brain *grows by use.* Providing an opportunity for baby to move in the water is an ideal way to develop not only a stronger body, but a better brain.

How does physical activity cause the brain to grow? The simple answer is *stimulation.* If a baby receives extraordinary stimulation, the brain will store an extraordinary amount of information. This is the foundation of human ability.

Swimming stimulates the brain's *sensory* areas. The back part of the brain is dedicated to incoming sensory information from our environment. This includes the visual (seeing), auditory (hearing), tactile (feeling), gustatory (tasting), and olfactory (smelling) senses. Everything we ever learn in our lifetime—everything Einstein ever learned in his lifetime—is the result of what the brain takes in through these five pathways.

All sensory stimulation requires a certain *frequency, intensity,* and *duration.* For example, one of the first words a baby learns is his own name. The baby hears his name more frequently, with greater intensity, and over a longer duration than any other name or word.

The front part of the brain is dedicated to outgoing *motor* commands used for mobility (body movement), language (talking), and manual competence (use of the hands). Everything we do with our muscles is accomplished through these three motor pathways. All these areas of the brain develop as a result of *opportunity*.

To have a complete understanding of how to fully develop all the sensory and motor areas of your baby's brain, read *How Smart Is Your Baby?* by my big sister, Janet Doman.

We can increase the development and growth of the sensory and motor areas of the brain by giving the newborn the opportunity to swim. The more opportunity we give the baby to move, the more his brain will develop and the more capable he will become.

After the marathon of birth and the many distractions that follow, there is often limited opportunity to swim in the baby's first days of life. In our family we solved this problem by making father responsible for baby's swimming. As a result, I enjoyed my own special time each day in the water with our babies.

In swimming, success depends almost entirely on ample opportunity. As such, swimming is an important—and fun—opportunity to develop a baby's brain from the earliest age.

# 2

## *Teaching Newborns to Swim*

As emphasized earlier, newborns already know how to swim. Since opportunity determines success, babies will succeed when given enough opportunity in the correct environment.

Moreover, as the magic is in the child and *not* the method, there is no single correct approach. Any method is successful if it results in a child who loves to swim and is safe in the water. As a child gains ability, he becomes safer in the water, but a truly safe child is always under the watchful eyes of a competent adult.

The purpose of this chapter is to outline a variety of successful "how-tos" for you and your baby. As a parent, you will discover what is most effective for you, your baby, and your family. If a technique works well for you, use it until it achieves its objective. Then go on to a more advanced technique. If, after a fair trial, a technique does not work for you and your baby, leave it and try another. Be creative. One of the joys of being in the water is discovering new activities that your baby loves.

Setting an example for your baby is a very important part of creating a successful swimming program. First and foremost, show your baby how much you love to be in the water. If your baby sees how happy mother is, he will understand that he can be happy, too.

Ideally, if you have an older child, cousin, or neighbor's child who loves to swim, take the child swimming with you. Babies watch older children attentively and want to do what the older child does. Whenever possible, have the older child demonstrate what you want the younger child to do, then do that activity with your baby. Apply this teaching technique for each chapter of the book. It will serve you well.

As an example of a typical program for newborns, I will explain the approach that I used with our baby, Noah, who began swimming on his first day of life.

Five important factors for teaching your newborn to swim include: *structure, time of day, feeding, location* and *method*.

## STRUCTURE THE BABY'S ENVIRONMENT

Many adults were hopelessly bored as children in school, where most classes and lessons were strictly controlled and repetitive. Some equate this structure with regimentation and boredom, but structure is good for the baby. The younger the baby, the more effective structure can be in the learning process. This is not a matter of educational technique, but of how the brain grows.

Alison Myers cuddles her 10-week-old daughter, Michaela, in a large bathtub.

The growth of sensory areas of the brain precedes the development of the motor areas. The newborn's sensory pathways are immature and need stimulation. The information acquired must be organized, since the baby lives in a highly chaotic world. If the external environment is organized, it helps the brain develop and improves the baby's ability to make sense of the world around him. For my children, I kept the bath area simple: soap, wash cloth, and towels. There were few visual and auditory distractions.

By organizing the environment, we make it easier for the baby to understand incoming information. As this occurs, the motor areas in the brain respond. For example, as the baby's vision improves, desire to move increases. Swimming is an ideal sensory and motor activity for newborns.

## TIME OF DAY

Create a schedule in which you swim with your baby at the same time each day. Noah and I always had our swimming session first thing in the morning in the bathtub. He was born in early April, before outdoor pools are opened, so there was no other option. It also gave me better control of the water temperature, which should be less than body temperature.

Noah learned rapidly that he had a date with me every morning. By three months of age he would smile and move his arms and body when I said, "Noah, are you ready to swim with father?"

## FEEDING

The issue of hunger and swimming is an important one. Many people believe they cannot swim immediately after eating, yet this is medically and scientifically unsound. In training, American sailors learn it is totally safe to get into the water right after a meal. For decades our mothers have been nursing their babies in the water before swimming sessions, keeping them well fed.

It is important for all children to avoid swimming when hungry. Food provides the energy and warmth needed to swim well.

## LOCATION

Swim in the same location and keep it organized in the same way each day. I always used the same bathtub and made sure the bath area was free of distractions. Noah quickly learned to identify the bath area as the place to swim.

## METHOD

The activities I did with Noah were presented to him in the same order each day. I would begin with activities that were easy for him and progress to those increasingly more difficult. Then I started the cycle over again, beginning with the easy activities.

By doing the same activities in the same order, Noah learned what he was going to do during each session. Gradually he began to understand the order. The more he understood, the more he enjoyed swimming.

Let's look at specific routines that can be incorporated into the baby's program.

## Cuddling

From the first day of life, I cuddled Noah as soon as we got into the water. This assured him that he was safe and loved, and that we were going to have a great time.

I was in a sitting position and slightly reclined, which permitted Noah to lie on me so we were face to face. The water level was up to my chest and shoulder blades. I encouraged him to put his feet on my upper thighs. Eventually he began to put weight on his feet and stand. At first he would only do this for a few seconds, but in time, for longer periods.

The purpose was to give him opportunity to be secure—initially just lying on me and eventually standing in a near-vertical position. By bearing more and more weight on

Noah Doman, age 10 weeks, and father hug in a Japanese bath.

his legs, his muscles became stronger. This ultimately would improve his kicking ability in the water and his ability to push with his legs when crawling on the floor.

## Balancing

After cuddling Noah, I was careful *not* to hold him as much. With his chin virtually on my shoulder, I was able to make sure he was safe and not sliding under the water. I could easily steady him before he took a mouthful of water. My objective was for him to learn to float and balance himself. If he lost balance, he could hold onto me.

Each day his balance improved. He learned to recover if he moved too far to the left or the right. He could grab me if he could not recover, or if he just felt like grabbing me. He eventually learned how to balance and float while lying on me.

Fourteen years earlier I taught Noah's oldest brother, Marlowe, how to float in the prone position. At that time we used an old-fashioned American bathtub. We made the bath as deep as possible and sometimes occluded the overflow opening to make it even deeper.

Marlowe was able to hold onto my knee and balance himself in the prone position. He loved to float and watch his friend, Chloe.

## Floating on the Back

From the first day of life Noah was unhappy on his back. He would feel disoriented and immediately became frightened. His breathing became shallow, fast, and irregular, and he assumed a spread eagle position. In every way he looked like someone falling backwards. This is not unusual for a newborn.

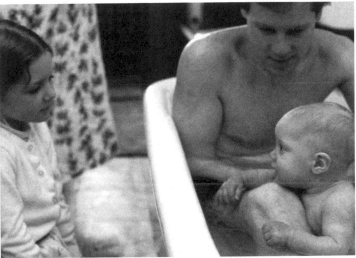

Marlowe Doman watches Chloe Coventry as he holds his father's knee and floats.

Our initial reaction might be to move the baby out of this position immediately. However, using a gentle step-by-step method, I could provide him with this important opportunity. I kept Noah in this position only until just before he would cry. I supported him by cupping the back of his head in my hand. His body floated freely. Then I cuddled him again so he could orient himself. After some days I learned that placing my other hand under his back, shoulders, legs, and other areas would help him to orient himself and stay on his back longer.

By the time he was two months of age, he began to tolerate being on his back longer. By his third month he was neutral about it, and by four months he was relaxed and thoroughly enjoying the position. He liked to kick and coo while floating on his back.

Noah happily floats on his back, with support.

I eventually tried to let go of him so he could float independently on his back, which some babies can do. There are even baby swimming programs that concentrate on teaching a baby how to float on his back in order to save himself should the baby accidentally fall into water. We agree that babies should be given the opportunity to learn how to float on their backs.

However, we also teach babies how to move through the water so that they can be as safe as possible.

## Blowing Bubbles

This is a simple and easy game I played with Noah to teach him to exhale into the water and to prevent him from inhaling water.

I began by lying on my back in the bathtub. The water level was deep enough so that I could easily lower my chin into the water and blow bubbles. I held Noah face to face with me, with his chin just above the water. At first I smiled and laughed, then showed him how to blow bubbles. I let him respond naturally, which at first included touching my mouth and the bubbles with his hands.

Noah watches father blow bubbles and blows some of his own.

After days or weeks of playing this game, your baby may try to blow a bubble. The baby's chin should be close enough to the water to allow him to try. At the sign of his first bubbles, praise the baby wildly. Alternate blowing bubbles—you, then the baby. You can be funny by changing the volume and tone while blowing out. The baby will love this.

In the 1970s a mother taught us that if you gently blow in your baby's face, the baby will reflexively hold his breath. If your baby is not breath holding when underwater, gently blow directly on the face, then carefully and quickly lower the baby into and out of water. Many mothers have found this a successful way of getting baby to breath hold.

## Bobbing Up and Down

Next I held Noah chin-deep in the water facing me, with my hands holding the sides of his chest just beneath his armpits. Then I raised him as high as I could over my head out of the water, then lowered him back into the water up to his chin. If you do this, be sure the air temperature in the room is not too cool.

Noah loved the feeling of flying out of the water and then

splashing back into it. Gradually he liked it more and more, occasionally uttering his first laughing sounds.

In time my movements became faster but
still controlled. Water would splash on Noah's
face and he loved it. As his ability to control
his breathing improved, I let his mouth go
into the water momentarily. My idea was that
he would learn to close his mouth. He had
another plan, however, which was to try to
drink the water.

Eventually he learned to go completely
under the water and hold his breath with this
activity. At times he would get some water
into his mouth and cough it out. When this
occurred, I waited until his breathing was regular and repeated the activity.

Noah holds his breath
briefly as he is lowered
into the water until his
mouth is covered.

This process can be made more gradual by first lowering the
baby to chin and mouth level, which helps baby learn not to inhale
water. Then lower the baby to the level of the nose until the same lesson is learned. Finally, the baby can be totally submersed in the
water.

Remember, what works great for one mother and baby may be
ineffective for another. What matters most is finding the successful
activities for you and your baby.

Babies who learn to hold their breath from bobbing up and down
can eventually be released in the water so they are free. The next step

Noah is chin-deep in the water.

Noah flies out of the water.

is to let the baby learn how to wiggle up through the water towards the surface. You will know precisely how long your baby can hold his breath, which is only a few seconds. Always be attentive and ready to pull the baby out of the water before he inhales water.

Ultimately, the baby will be able to go completely underwater and rise to the surface to take a breath.

## Putting Baby Under a Gentle Shower

One technique is to pass the baby under a gentle shower of water to teach him breath holding. This technique is done on a gentle gradient that eventually gives the baby the ability to go underwater.

*Ninety percent of swimming success is dependent upon learning how to control breathing when underwater.* The problem is that when the face is submerged, water will naturally flow into the nose and mouth and baby will cough. How can we avoid this and teach the baby to hold his breath?

There are three ways to do this while holding the baby upright.

1.  Begin with a tiny volume of water flowing from the showerhead. Begin with so little water that the baby's head barely gets wet and there's no risk of taking in water.

2.  Increase the speed of passing the baby under the shower. Perform this gently, smoothly, and quickly. Again, the baby may barely get wet and not inhale water. The faster the motion, the less volume of water will hit the baby's face. However, be careful not to use abrupt or jerky movements, as these would be unpleasant for the baby.

3.  Start by having the shower water fall on the back or side of the baby's head. Little water will flow over his nose or mouth. Gradually move the center of the baby's head toward the center of the shower. Eventually pass the baby's head under the center of the shower so he receives the maximum volume of water.

Utilize these three methods to create a very gentle process whereby the volume of water on the baby's face gradually increases. Ideally this process should be so gradual that baby does not realize it is happening. Slowly the baby will learn breath control.

The more times baby goes under the shower in a given session, the more quickly breath holding will be learned. During Noah's first

Father says, "One, two, three. . . ." as he moves Noah towards the sprinkling water.

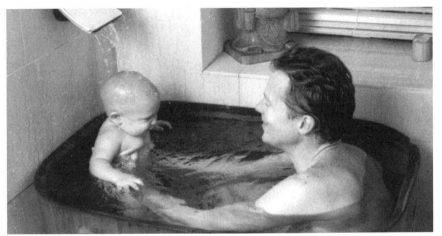

When father says "under," Noah passes under the sprinkling water.

Noah loves the water.

week of life, I began by putting him under the shower only once in a swimming session. Next I put him under two times in a row, then three times, then four, and so on, up to ten nonstop passes. By the third week of life we built up to ten passes in a session.

From the first week I followed an exact routine for each session. I adjusted the volume of the water flow from the shower so it was very slight. I made sure Noah's breathing was good, and that he was attentive and content. Holding him under his armpits and having him face me, I said, "Noah, I am going to count to three, then put you under the shower, so hold your breath. Here we go!" As I passed him toward the shower I counted, "One, two, three, under!" Precisely as I said "under," his head went under the shower. The baby learns more easily and quickly when you say the exact same phrase with sufficient frequency, intensity, and duration.

This process programs the sensory areas of the brain to learn breath holding. As Noah passed under the shower he could *feel* (via the tactile pathway to the brain) the water rolling down his face. He could *see* (via the visual pathway) the water dropping onto his eyes and then into the bath. He could *hear* (via the auditory pathway) the water coming out of the faucet, running down over his ears and falling into the bath. He could *taste* the water running into his

Marlowe, at three months, anticipates going underwater when father says "three."

mouth, and to some extent even *smell* the water. The simultaneous stimulation of all five sensory areas of the brain is the most effective and efficient way to program the brain. This is one reason that newborns are able to learn so quickly to control their breathing.

Each time Noah went under the shower, his brain learned an important lesson about breathing. By the third week of life I had built up to ten passes under the shower in a row. Between each pass I paused for a few seconds to make sure his breathing was regular. If it was not, I paused long enough for it to become regular and to make sure he was attentive and content. Then I started again. I held him facing me and said, "One, two, three, under."

The method of counting was "one, two, three, under," "*two*, two, three, under," "*three*, two, three, under"—all the way up to "*ten*, two, three, under." This gave Noah enough time to hold his breath before going under. He also became familiar with counting and eventually understood how many times he was going under.

By the fourth week I gradually built up to two groups of ten consecutive passes under the shower, and gradually added a third group of ten by the fifth week. If I managed to swim with Noah once each day of the week, he would have hundreds of opportunities to learn breath holding!

## Moving in the Horizontal Position

As soon as the baby is comfortable, it is important for him to be in a horizontal position when placed under the shower. In this position, gravity pulls water away from the nose and mouth more quickly and it's more difficult to inhale water.

For all of the activities, keep the baby in the horizontal position, face down towards the water, as much as possible. Swimming in a vertical position is very inefficient and makes learning more difficult.

In a typical American bathroom, the position of the showerhead high on the wall above the bathtub makes it difficult to pass the baby under it and then in the water while horizontal. In some cases, you can use the faucet of the bathtub—however, this may also be difficult. The best alternative is to purchase an inexpensive rubber showerhead with an adapter so it can be attached to either the showerhead pipe or the faucet. The photos on page 21 show a white tube connected to the faucet of the bathtub. These can usually be purchased at a hardware store (see Appendix).

Mother gently moves Michaela towards the sprinkling water.

Water sprinkles on the back of Michaela's head.

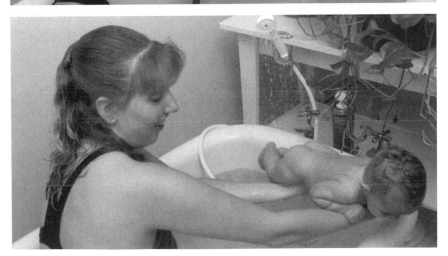

Mother moves Michaela away from the showerhead, while keeping her in the horizontal position.

## Submerging the Baby

Depending on the type of bathtub, there are different ways that new-borns can be submerged. Typical American bathtubs are long but not deep. Mother can be most comfortable sitting up, with her back resting against the back wall of the bath.

To submerge the baby in this type of tub, hold the baby under the armpits with the baby facing away from you. Lean over so you can see your baby's face well. Explain to your baby what you are going to do. Attentively observe the baby's breathing and count, "One, two, three, under." When you say "under," gently move the baby in the horizontal position, and briefly put the baby under the water.

Your goal is to submerge the baby's entire face momentarily, but you may choose to start on a gentler gradient. At first, submerge only the baby's mouth. Obviously, it is best if baby keeps his mouth closed. In time, submerge baby's mouth and nose. Finally, submerge baby's entire face.

Another technique is to combine passing the baby horizontally under the shower with horizontally submerging the baby's face under the water.

Newborns can learn to hold their breath in the bath.

Baby goes
underwater
for a second.

Baby emerges
from the water
and is fine.

Father says, "One, two, three, under," and Noah moves under the shower.

Noah passes under the water for an instant.

He comes up for kisses and hugs.

This is what I did with Noah in the Japanese bath. By the third week Noah was going under the shower ten times with a brief pause between each pass. When he could do this without difficulty, I stopped and congratulated him after the tenth pass under the shower. Then I would say: "Noah, this time I am going to count to three, put you under the shower, and then under the water. Here we go!" The grand finale of each of Noah's swimming sessions was to be completely submerged.

As I said "under," his head passed under the shower. After observing his breathing and seeing that he was content, I counted again "one, two, three, under" and put him under the water in the tub.

Whether he came out of the water breathing regularly or sputtering I always smiled, told him what a great swimmer he was, and kissed and hugged him. Because this was potentially the most difficult part of the session, I would then return to one of the easiest parts, such as cuddling.

Each time I added a group of ten passes under the shower, I added another opportunity to go completely underwater at the end. By the end of the fifth week, he was up to three groups of ten passes under the shower and three opportunities to be completely submerged.

## Making Sessions Genki

*Genki* is a great word that our Japanese staff members have taught us. In Japanese it means a combination of being happy, healthy, energetic, and enthusiastic. This is a very important part of teaching your newborn to swim. Make each session genki.

My swimming sessions with Noah did not always go well. Some days he did very well and some days he occasionally sputtered under the shower or came up choking. These less successful days were discouraging. My wife, Rosalind, told me I was getting *too* serious and too concerned. She reminded me of the meaning of *genki*.

Enthusiasm and energy can be contagious. I was expecting each session to be perfect. From that day on, Noah improved even more. Remembering the meaning of *genki*, I cheered and clapped about *everything* Noah did. By his third month of life, he was having the perfect sessions I had hoped for. He rarely had a problem, and when he did, he did not care and made it clear that he wanted to continue. Passing him under the shower was working and so I reduced the passes from three groups of ten to three groups of five. Each group continued to be followed by a trip completely underwater, which he did very well.

A joyous swimming session for Noah and father.

## "Jumping" into the Bath

Eventually your baby will learn to sit on the side of the pool and "jump" in. Initially, as you stand in the pool, you will hold the baby's hands and gently ease the baby into the water. To prepare for the pool, we can simulate this process at home in the bath.

Providing the rim of the bath is wide enough, you can sit baby on the rim with baby's feet in the bath. The bath should be filled as deep as possible. As you sit comfortably in the bath, hold baby's left hand with your right hand and baby's right hand with your left hand. Then slowly ease baby into the bath with you.

Japanese baths have no rim. They have the advantage of being deep, and the water goes right up to the top of the side. Luckily in my case the windowsill is next to the bath and we could use it for Noah to "jump" into the bath.

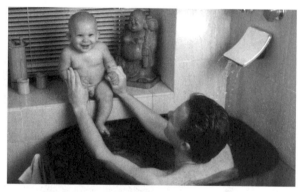

Noah gets ready to jump into a traditional Japanese bath.

Noah is gently carried into the water.

Noah holds his breath briefly, while father makes certain he is happy.

Babies love these activities and will do them over and over again.

## Holding onto the Side

An advantage to a Japanese-style bath such as mine is that the side is thin enough that a newborn can grasp and hold it. When I first took Noah into the bath at birth, he could use his natural grasp reflex to hold onto the side with a little support from me.

Well babies are born with a grasp reflex. When an object such as a pencil or an adult's finger is placed securely in a newborn's palm, the baby automatically grasps it.

This is a *developmental* reflex, meaning that as a child develops the reflex is lost. Since manual competence is a motor function of the brain, the key to developing manual abilities is opportunity. The more a newborn grasps, the sooner this reflex is no longer needed, and the sooner the next, more sophisticated manual ability develops.

I would open Noah's tightly fisted hands and place them over the smooth wooden side of the Japanese bath. The water came up to Noah's shoulder blades and supported a considerable amount of his weight. For about the first two weeks I held my hand on his bottom in case he slipped off into the water. He learned to hold his chin on the top of the tub, which helped anchor him in place. Gradually I withdrew my hand until he was hanging independently. I was very impressed with his rapid manual development.

Noah, twelve weeks old, holds himself up by grasping the side of the bath.

The next step of manual development is called *vital release.* The baby learns to let go as the grasp reflex disappears.

The problem is that too many babies develop manual opportunity by accident, which slows overall development. In the bath we can give baby lots of opportunity and therefore accelerate his manual development. The joy of manipulating objects in the bath will make the baby happy. Most importantly the baby is growing and developing areas of the brain responsible for manual function.

Within a few weeks Noah was able to let go of the tub. When babies reach this stage they often cannot hold on as well, because the grasp reflex no longer exists. As a result, they often lose the opportunity to hold on with their fingers until such time as their strength improves.

I expected Noah would no longer hold onto the side of the bath, but I was wrong. He learned to teethe on the top of the smooth wooden sides. He also liked drinking the water as it flowed past his mouth! By one month of age he could hold on for a minute. With each passing month his ability improved by about a minute. At three months he could hold onto the side for three minutes.

This feat required balance, because his feet could not touch the bottom of the bath, and strength. He had to hold himself well enough that he did not float away.

Noah rapidly developed to the next level of manual proficiency—*prehensile grasp*. This is the ability to reach out and pick up an

object. By the end of his third month I no longer had to pry his fingers open and place them over the side of the bath. As I turned him to the side he reached out to grasp it. Initially, I helped guide his hands, but he learned to grasp the side independently.

## Holding onto Thumbs

It is not necessary to have a Japanese bath to develop your baby's manual competence. In a typical American bath, sit and lean your back against the wall. Sit baby on your thighs facing you. Put your thumb or index fingers in baby's palms. The baby should hold onto your fingers tightly. Open your legs and gently lower

Michaela, ten weeks old, grasps mother's thumbs and stands in the bathtub.

baby into the water, which should be as deep as possible.

The deeper the water, the more it will support baby's weight, and the easier and longer he will hold on. As you feel baby's grip loosen, be prepared to hold him with your fingers. If necessary, block the overflow opening of the bath, in order to make the water deeper.

Another possibility is to allow your baby to stand on the floor of the bath as the baby grasps your thumbs. As noted earlier, standing can help him develop balance and strength. Without these opportunities it may take the baby longer to learn to swim.

## In the Pool

Providing the water and air temperatures are warm enough, and the water is devoid of harmful chemicals, newborn babies can swim outside in pools. The same methods described above for submerging the baby underwater can be continued in the pool. The baby can be submerged horizontally, as we do in a typical American bath, or the baby can be submerged vertically, as I did with my children in the Japanese bath.

By three months of age, Noah was happily sitting on the side of the pool, and either with help or independently would jump into the pool and swim out to me. In the beginning, I would permit him to be underwater for only a few seconds before I would grasp him under the armpits and pull him out of the water to hug me.

As he learned to hold his breath longer, he would swim farther and farther out to me. The air in a baby's body naturally causes the body to rise to the surface. In time I would let him start to rise before I eased him out of the water. Eventually he began to kick his way to the surface as well, and then I would pull him into my arms.

Noah sits on the edge of the pool and jumps into the water with father's help.

Noah swims out to father.

Father grabs Noah under the armpits and praises him for his achievement.

## SUMMARY

There are two objectives of this program. First and foremost is for the baby to love being in the water. The second is for the baby to learn breath holding under the water. Providing these objectives are achieved while the baby is young, it is almost impossible to fail. Loving the water and controlling one's breathing are the fundamentals upon which all swimming is based.

The only threat to success is a lack of opportunity. As long as the baby has enough opportunity to swim, improvement will continue.

We must never forget that the magic is in the child. As parents we need to maintain our enthusiasm, and give the baby's sensory pathways frequent input about how it feels to go underwater and hold the breath.

Use the activities in this chapter with high frequency in each swimming session. Swim daily if possible. Be consistent from week to week. These are essential for learning. Remember, two weeks of missed swimming in the life of an eight-week-old is twenty-five percent of the baby's life!

Be creative. Use these activities but also create your own. All babies are unique—find out what your baby likes and pursue it with enthusiasm.

Father helps Noah go underwater.

He guides Noah through the water.

A friend waits attentively to help Noah to the surface.

# Checklist for Newborns

**Before swimming make sure baby is fed and rested.**

- ☐ Frequent cuddling, with hugs and kisses.
- ☐ Balancing and floating with baby's chin on mother's shoulder.
- ☐ Floating on the back.
- ☐ Blowing bubbles.
- ☐ Bobbing up and down.
- ☐ Passing under a gentle shower (up to 10 times nonstop).
- ☐ Going underwater.
- ☐ Passing under a shower followed by going underwater (after the tenth pass under the shower).
- ☐ Jumping into the bath or pool.
- ☐ Grasping the side of the tub or mother's thumbs.
- ☐ Always end with lots of hugs and kisses.

Because of the difficulty of holding a baby while trying to read a book, we have created waterproof swimming program checklists that mothers can wear on their wrists in the bath or pool. See Resources in the back of the book.

# 3

## *Teaching Six- to Twelve-Month-Olds to Swim*

As your baby continues to develop and outgrows the bath, there needs to be a *gradual* transition to a pool or open water. Most babies can continue to swim in the bath until about six months of age, and tiny babies until about nine months. If the baby is just too big for the bath, you will have to make this transition more quickly, or arrange for a larger tub. If your baby has no problems with an indoor pool, simply proceed with your swimming program there.

As the baby outgrows the bath, slowly decrease swimming in that location and increase time in the pool or open water. For example, swim four days a week in the bath and one day in a pool, gradually exchanging one day per week of swimming in the bath for swimming in the pool. After one month of this, all swimming will be in a pool. Such a schedule can be lengthened to suit your baby's needs. The objective is maximum opportunity for your baby to swim. You and your baby's favorite part of the day just may be going to the pool.

The unlimited opportunity afforded by tropical or warm weather environments can only be fully appreciated by those of us who live in colder environments. In Philadelphia, outdoor pools are only open four to five months a year. There are few options available other than indoor pools. This led our Russian friends to create alternatives such as large plexiglass baths. The Appendix contains information about other types of baths and small pools.

One disadvantage of indoor commercial pools is they are often too cold for babies. If this is the case, you have the option of finding a pool that is warm, or creating an environment at home as noted above. Such an environment may serve you well until your child is old enough to tolerate the cooler temperatures of the local pool, which may be at around eighteen months to two years of age.

Because of the very large selection of small, medium, and large home pools available, it is relatively easy to find one that works well for your family. Small home pools can be set up in enclosed porches, basements, or garages during cool weather. Both the air and water can be kept warm. Home pools permit you to clean the water without harmful chemicals.

In a warm climate, maximize your baby's opportunity by swimming outside whenever possible.

Babies who have been swimming since birth will love swimming in a pool. After watching the older children, your baby will push you for more activities. Getting your child out of the pool becomes increasingly difficult each day.

Also, as the baby swims more, the heart and lungs will develop, the breath will be held longer, and the chest will grow. The baby's muscles will also grow stronger. Overall, mobility will develop, as will language and manual competence. As the baby develops, the immune system will be better equipped to handle indoor commercial pools.

Babies who grow up in a warm environment near natural open water, such as a lake or the ocean, learn that water is a playground. In these environments, swim when the water is relatively calm. Babies react to warm, calm open water as they do to the bath.

## IN THE POOL

Many elements of the program for the newborn baby can be continued in the pool. The baby will be happy to swim in any environment in which he feels safe and protected.

The objective of this program is to continue the newborn program in the pool, providing the baby already enjoys swimming and is breath holding underwater.

The key to success remains providing the maximum opportunity to swim.

In this part of the program we will gradually extend the length of time the baby is able to go underwater and hold his breath. With each passing month, the baby should be able to hold his breath longer. At about twelve months of age, the baby should be able to sit on the side of the pool, jump into the water, swim a few feet underwater, and come to the surface for a breath—all with little or no assistance. There are six activities to help bring about these wonderful abilities.

Even at ten weeks of age, Michaela enjoys an outdoor pool.

Noah is ready to swim to Alison.

After "One, two, three, under," he goes underwater with a gentle push.

He kicks and moves through the water.

Alison brings him to the surface and says, "Bravo!"

## Cuddling

Any mother who has been in the bath with her baby does not need to be reminded to hug and love her baby while in the pool. This comes naturally. Use cuddling to praise the baby for all he accomplishes and as a break when rest is needed. As he improves, the baby will demand more and more swimming.

## Floating on the Back

Continue providing opportunity for the baby to float on his back exactly as you did in the bath. This can sometimes be used as a rest period between opportunities to go under the water. Increasingly permit your baby to float independently, slowly reducing your support over time. Eventually the baby should be floating more independently without being aware of it.

Some babies are capable of floating independently for minutes, while some are not. However, it is important that the baby enjoys the position, learns to balance himself, and becomes able to float with less and less support.

Noah learns to float as father supports his head.

## Going Underwater

This is the single most important activity at this level. We are developing the baby's ability for breath holding and staying underwater longer. In the pool there are many different ways we can do this, and babies love all of them. The following methods can be organized into a sequence of activities.

### *Swimming to Mother*

In the bath it is not really possible for the baby to swim to you because of space, but not so in the pool. Standing about chest-deep in the water, facing the baby, hold him under the armpits and walk backwards. As much as possible keep the baby in the prone, or horizontal, position. (Babies, like adults, if they do not kick, will naturally fall into the vertical position instead of remaining horizontal.) For babies and children of all ages, keeping one's body in the horizontal position is very important.

Walk backward in order to create a gentle current of water that will help the baby move forward and maintain a horizontal position. Constantly monitor the baby's face.

When baby is ready to go underwater, give the "one, two, three, under" command. Gently release and allow the baby to go underwater very briefly. After baby surfaces, hug, kiss, and praise your baby for being a great swimmer.

As babies improve they can stay underwater for longer periods. Eventually, move backwards more quickly so the water current you create, your *wake*, helps keep the baby moving and in the horizontal position.

Mother walks backwards, preparing Michaela to go underwater.

Still walking backwards, mother gently eases Michaela under the water.

Hugs for Michaela as she comes out of the water.

## *Swimming Between Mother and Father*

Another activity in waist-deep water is to hold the baby underneath the armpits but facing away from you and towards another person. Use the command "one, two, three, under" or whatever is appropriate. Baby is placed underwater and gently passed to the other person. Pushing too fast may force water into the baby's mouth. The other person should take hold of baby under the armpits, raise the baby up out of the water, and give hugs and kisses.

When first performing this activity, the other person may grasp the baby before you let go. In this case, the baby is underwater only for a moment. With better breath holding, the baby can stay underwater for longer periods and travel farther.

Alison says to Michaela, "One, two, three . . ."

". . . Under," says mother.

After months of doing this activity consistently and with ease, you may push the baby through the water farther and faster in the horizontal position. However, do this in moderation because we eventually want the baby to learn to propel himself through the water by kicking.

When this activity becomes routine, the other person, following the exact same procedure, should send the baby back to you. After the appropriate cuddling and kissing, and making sure the baby's breathing is regular, pass the baby back again to your partner. As the baby's swimming improves, increase the frequency of swimming between two people. Always stop and go onto another activity *before* the baby wants to stop, so that baby remains eager to continue.

Mother guides Michaela towards Douglas.

Michaela is thrilled and Douglas congratulates her.

### Jumping In

As you stand in water about chest-deep, sit the baby on the edge of the pool. Put your index fingers inside the baby's hands. Encourage the baby to jump into the water with a "one, two, three" count or other command.

Some babies will immediately jump into the water without your help. Others will need the encouragement and a gentle pull. Lovingly allow your baby to enter the water. Let the baby go underwater only briefly and back to the surface, facing you the entire time. Give the baby hugs, kisses, and congratulations for being such a great swimmer.

A swimsuit may protect well enough, but if baby is bare and if

Noah grasps
father's thumbs.

Noah goes gently
into the water.

the edge of the pool is rough, consider placing a tiny piece of smooth material under baby's bottom.

With opportunity the baby will become more independent at jumping into the water. The goal is for this to become so enjoyable that the baby jumps in whenever the opportunity arises—another strong reason for your absolute vigilance at all times.

As this activity evolves, the baby will jump into the water more forcefully. This will help the baby to develop faster movement in the water and to more easily reach the horizontal position. Obviously you will need to step back as the baby jumps and swims farther out into the pool. With better breath holding, the baby will eventually stay underwater longer and swim farther.

Father moves backwards as Noah moves forward.

Hugs for the swimming boy.

## Climbing Out

Although in the beginning it is virtually impossible for a six-month-old to climb out of a pool independently, it is vitally important to teach this skill as early as possible. This is an important safety skill. Unfortunately, the water level of most pools ranges from six to twelve inches below the deck of the pool.

Standing in chest-deep water, hold your baby under the armpits or by the sides, facing the side of the pool. Encourage the baby to grab the edge of the pool and do as much of the work as possible. Place one hand on the baby's bottom for a delicate push. If necessary,

Noah, at five months, holds onto the side of the pool.

Noah pulls himself up while father supports his bottom.

Noah is halfway out of the pool.

Noah starts to creep away.

use your other hand to help the baby place his hands and elbows on the deck and crawl out of the pool. Continue to push until the baby is entirely out of the pool and on the deck. Gradually reduce your help as the baby becomes more independent.

There are some pools where the edge is almost level with the water. Fortunately we happened upon such a pool when Noah was fifteen months old. After being helped out of the pool once, he was able to climb out by himself. He loved it and became more confident with this new skill.

In open water, all these activities may be performed with a floating raft or smooth dock close to the water's surface.

## Blowing Bubbles

Just as we began blowing bubbles with the newborn in the bath, we can continue the same game in a pool. Hold the baby under the armpits, facing you, and blow bubbles. Encourage the baby to do the same. Play the game of taking turns—you blow bubbles, then the baby. Laugh, hug, and kiss frequently. Create similar games of making sounds with the bubbles. For example, buy a whistle and play the game of blowing it under the water. Bubbles will come out of it along with a funny sound. Teach the baby how to do it, too. This helps further develop control of breathing.

Mother blows bubbles while Michaela watches in fascination.

## Bobbing Up and Down

Continue with this activity. By now your baby will be briefly breath holding when underwater. With improvement, gradually let baby stay underwater longer.

The previous activities should be done frequently in the course of a swimming session. Use these activities and add others that you discover with your baby.

Remember the importance of structure. You can now organize a sequence of activities. Like the program for newborns, start with the activities that are easy and progress to more challenging ones. You might begin by doing one activity once, and go onto the next and the next. Then start over again with cuddling.

Gradually build up the number of times you do this sequence during a session in the water. High frequency with brief duration of each activity is the key to growing the sensory areas of your baby's brain while improving swimming.

Marlowe, at age one, loves to swim underwater with father at the end of each swimming lesson.

## About Play

Play is an integral part of any swimming lesson. However, we have found that it is best to begin pool time with a lesson that includes all of the previous activities. These provide the neurological and physical basis for successful swimming. Joy, fun, and playing around are all essential to the lesson.

Once the activities are done with appropriate frequency, the lesson part of the swimming session is over and the play part can begin. Babies use the skills learned in the lesson as part of their play, and parents create play activities that can be incorporated into future swimming sessions.

# Checklist for Six- to Twelve-Month-Olds

☐ Frequent cuddling, with hugs and kisses.

☐ Floating on the back.

☐ Swimming to mother.

☐ Swimming between mother and father.

☐ Jumping into the water from the side of the pool.

☐ Climbing out.

☐ Blowing bubbles.

☐ Bobbing up and down.

☐ Giving hugs and kisses.

As baby improves, gradually repeat any of the above activities. In time, repeat as frequently as you and your baby wish.

# 4

# *Water Safety and Hygiene*

As your child transitions to pools or open water and becomes a more capable and independent swimmer, safety, hygiene, and adult vigilance is vital. *We cannot be too careful about a child's safety around water.*

At The Institutes, in our work with brain-injured children, we have seen tiny children who scaled fences around a pool, children who unlocked doors that adults could not, and children who almost drowned in a few inches of water on a pool cover. We have seen every kind of tragedy that can befall children, but few compare with those of a near-drowning accident.

It is important to be ever vigilant and establish rules related to water safety and hygiene. Even newborns rapidly learn to understand verbal instructions such as "one, two, three, under." It's never too early to start talking safety. Moreover, it is our responsibility to teach children a profound *respect* for the water.

## POOL CHEMICALS

Before discussing important safety and hygiene factors, it is necessary to highlight the issue of chlorine and other pool chemicals.

Chlorine and other chemicals are used in many home and commercial pools. It is always best to avoid exposure to these chemicals since most people have some sensitivity to them, especially babies. This may include respiratory problems, eye and skin irritation, and allergic reactions. Since chlorine evaporates from water it is especially bad during a shower or bath because the vapors are inhaled and chlorine compounds enter the body through the lungs. You can smell this evaporated chlorine in rooms with indoor pools, or even in your own shower.

A filter that removes chlorine can be used to prevent chlorinated water from entering your home. There are also water filters for drinking and bathing taps. For pools there are many options, the best of which is salt water. These are discussed in the Appendix.

There are babies who have absolutely no problem transitioning, even in the middle of wintertime, from the bath to an indoor pool.

We learned about chlorine the hard way. When our first son outgrew the bathtub we took him to the local public pool. He was swimming superbly at home at two months of age, but the more he swam in the public pool the greater was his allergic reaction to the chemicals, and the more difficult it was for him to progress.

Chlorine can be a very harmful substance for your child. Showering, as discussed on page 50, can help rinse off some of these chemicals when they are in the water. Consider the many options, such as converting your existing pool to salt water, or buying a small plastic pool or a relatively inexpensive larger pool. Almost all pools can use salt water, ozone, or other safe chemicals, as mentioned in the Appendix.

## WATER RULES

You can be more certain of your children's safety in the water if they are with you or another competent adult. The most important rule is that young children should *never* be in the water alone. In addition, you need to be your child's lifeguard, as safety is the top priority.

Here are some other important water rules:

### Prepare the Swimming Environment

In the same way the newborn was taught how a swimming session is organized, we should teach children from the earliest age that their lessons are organized. You can involve your child in organizing the goggles and kickboards before the swim, or other equipment such as towels or clothes for after the swim.

The child also learns that preparation is part of swimming and is good for safety. It also helps teach the child not to dash into the water ahead of you. As swimming becomes more advanced or when there are two or more children in the family, this becomes increasingly important. Each child must be taught that safety is his responsibility.

## Children Should Only Enter the Water with a Parent

From the earliest age, children who love to swim want to get into the water often and for as long as possible. When near an inviting body of water, their first response is to jump in.

It is vital that you teach your child never to get in the water without you, and that you are absolutely in command at all times. If you are not ready to get into the water for whatever reason, baby must know to wait until you invite him into the water. This rule should be strictly followed.

## Children Should Respect a Sibling's Lesson

With two or more children, you may want to take turns teaching each child. The others must sit patiently until you are ready to teach them. You should always have all of your children in sight when you are in or near water.

## Children Should Walk, Not Run, Near the Pool

Children who love to swim are always excited about getting into the pool. Wet concrete or tile floors can be very slippery and falls occur easily. There is also the possibility of accidentally falling into the water, which coupled with hitting one's head can have severe consequences.

## Dive Only in Water that Is Deep Enough

For diving in typical pools the YMCA requires a depth of 5 feet (1.52m) from the surface of the water to the bottom of the pool. USA Swimming requires a minimum depth of 4 feet (1.22m) from the surface to the bottom. Obviously, the distance from the deck of the pool to the water surface is an additional factor for consideration.

## Children Clean Up After Swimming

By establishing this rule, the child knows that the swimming session has ended and that he may not get back into the pool. Just as in the preparation, even young children should have some clean-up responsibility. Depending on their ages, some children can put towels back into the bag, retrieve the kickboard, or put away the goggles as you supervise.

## HEALTH

Before going to swim, a child should be fed, well rested, and healthy. If baby is sick, has an elevated temperature (even a mild fever), has been fighting off a cold, or is just recovering from an illness, it is not the time to go swimming.

### Showering

Both mother and child should shower *before* and *after* going into a public pool. Unhealthy bacteria can mix with the pool water, which requires that more chemicals be added to keep the pool water hygienic. If you detect a foul odor in the air around the pool, it may be a sign of too much bacteria in the water. In addition, if you smell too much chlorine or chemicals in pool water, it can be indicative of the same. Neither environment is ideal for swimming.

In order to help neutralize the chlorine and chemicals, rinse the hair with a mild solution of water and lemon juice or distilled vinegar. When swimming in open water, showering afterwards helps rinse off dirt and sand, bacteria, parasites, salt, and other foreign matter.

Samuel Weinglass, age six, wears goggles as he swims on his back.

### Eye Protection

At an early age, a child may begin using goggles. The first pair should be given with great fanfare so that your child learns that this is an important piece of equipment, not a toy. Goggles can be worn for a few minutes initially and gradually for longer periods until the child is accustomed to them. Ideally, parents, siblings, or older friends should set an example by wearing goggles before they are given to the child. This way the child looks forward to the day when he can have goggles, too.

There are several advantages to using goggles besides protecting the eyes from chemicals. They make swimming more interesting because your child can now see around the entire pool, lake, or ocean. Goggles also help the child stay oriented, and reduce the possibility of drifting into deep water. The child can see you, the wall, and the bottom of the pool, and is more confident as a result. An added benefit is that when big sister is playing "shark" and attacking from under the water, she can be spotted more easily.

## Water-Related Illnesses

In addition to chlorine and pool chemicals, there are three common water risks that apply to adults, children, and babies.

1. *Diarrhea Illnesses:* These are due to chlorine-resistant organisms, poor facility maintenance, and unhealthy habits (not showering before and after swimming, evacuating the bladder or bowel into the water). These risks are usually confined to public pools.

2. *Swimmer's Itch:* This is usually limited to lakes where certain parasites can cause an itchy inflammation in the skin. Symptoms begin about 48 hours after exposure and may last seven days. A red, pinpoint rash is the classic sign. It often goes away on its own but severe or persistent cases may require medical attention.

3. *Ear Infections:* At one time, swimming was blamed for causing ear infections. However, middle ear infections are not associated with swimming. External canal infections are more common in swimmers. In this case, swimming should be avoided until the infection is gone. To prevent ear infections after swimming, clean the outside of the ears with a mix of 50% pure water and 50% distilled vinegar. Do not push cotton into the ears.

Basic first aid, which is beyond the scope of this book, should also be part of your education. In all, water safety and hygiene should be a key focus for you and an important part of the child's swimming education.

# Water Safety and Hygiene Checklist

☐ Control the cleanliness of the water, water temperature, air temperature, and safety. There are many small, inexpensive home pools for both inside and outside the house. Avoid unnecessary pool chemicals.

☐ Make sure children are fed, rested, and have gone to the bathroom before swimming.

☐ Water and air should be sufficiently warm.

☐ Teach children to prepare the swimming environment.

☐ Shower before swimming in public pools.

☐ Children should enter the water only when a parent says it is safe to do so.

☐ Children should walk, not run, in the pool area.

☐ Children should always be in your sight.

☐ Children can help to keep the swim safe.

☐ Children wear goggles when appropriate.

☐ Children should clean up after swimming.

☐ Shower after swimming in public pools.

**Goal:** For children to have a profound respect for the water.

*SAFETY IS THE NUMBER ONE PRIORITY.*

# 5

## *Teaching One- to Two-Year-Olds to Swim*

This program is for children who can perform all the activities in the previous chapter. It can be used in a pool, lake, or gentle ocean.

By now the child is a swimmer, and increasing the activities in the pool will promote the child's physical development. The principles you have learned remain as important as ever:

- Cuddling, kissing, and joyousness are integral parts of swimming.

- Maintain frequent opportunity. Do each activity briefly and then go on to another.

- Maintain the structure of each swimming session. When, where, and how should remain as consistent as possible.

- You and your child should understand the rules of the water (previously discussed) and apply them consistently.

The objective of this part of the program is that by age two the child can do the following *independently:*

1. Climb out of the pool.

2. Swim the width of a pool independently (approximately 6 yards or meters). This means the child can swim underwater for a few feet, rise to the surface to take a breath, then swim underwater for a few feet and rise again, etc.

3. Safely dive into the pool.

If your swimming environment is a lake or gentle ocean, the objective would be to have the child walk into the water with you from the beach, swim out a short distance to you, turn around, swim back, and walk out of the water onto the beach. However, loud crashing waves can scare some babies and you may have to introduce them to the water much more gradually. Strong winds, cooler air, and rough water may also be frightening at first.

Setting a positive example for your child is essential. Children want to do everything older kids do. However, sometimes older children can set a negative example. We need to protect children from examples that may lead to dangers or risks.

Accomplishing the three objectives on page 53 is a tremendous victory. It means the child has the basics of swimming and water safety. However, it does not mean the child can be independent or safe in the water without you.

The following program is comprised of twelve activities. For the child to learn them well, he should do them frequently.

When you are consistently doing all twelve activities, your child may try to get you to do them over again. In the beginning resist this and end the session *before* the child wants to stop to avoid fatigue. As endurance improves, you can gradually increase the frequency of the activities.

As previously discussed, your child should be responsible for preparing to swim when you arrive at the swimming environment. Bring the child into the water, cuddle, and play until you are both comfortable and ready to swim.

## A TYPICAL SWIMMING SESSION

In the beginning, you may do only the first five or six activities. Gradually include all twelve in each swimming session.

## 1. Holding the Side of the Pool

An important prerequisite for climbing out of the pool independently is learning to hold the edge of the pool. Give your child plenty of opportunity to do this until the child can hold on for minutes with ease. This activity will be coupled with #2 on page 55, pushing off the side after holding on for a short period of time.

## 2. Pushing Off the Side

While holding onto the side of the pool independently, invite your child to push off and swim to you. At first this may only be a few inches. Eventually, the child will learn to go faster and farther, especially by using the feet to push off. As with the other activities, give your child opportunity to swim longer distances to you.

Mason Zeberlein, age two, holds onto the side of the pool, preparing to push off with his feet and swim to mother.

Mason swims away from the wall as mother waits for him.

Mason swims to mother.

Mother greets him.

Father gives Noah,
seventeen months,
a push to the steps.

## 3. Swimming to the Steps

Standing near the steps, gently push your child underwater toward them. Perhaps the child travels one foot through the water to arrive at the steps. In shallow water, it's best to be on your knees, or in a squatting or sitting position. At a beach, gently push your child into shallower water.

At first you will have to help the child learn to stand up onto the step or beach. With time, the child will want to do this independently.

Over the next few weeks, gradually move farther from the steps so the child can swim farther and more independently.

Noah
approaches
the steps.

Noah begins
to walk up
the steps.

## 4. Floating on the Back

An important objective is for children to learn how to float on their backs independently. If your child can do this for a few seconds, continue building up the nonstop floating time to a minute or more.

## 5. Swimming from the Steps

While you are in the water, encourage the child to swim to you from the steps. Initially you may offer a hand, but gradually move farther away. As your child's swimming improves, gradually move even farther away.

This will help the child improve breath holding, respiration, and physical endurance. Since swimming stimulates further brain development, functions such as language can be improved as a result.

Noah jumps in from the steps and swims to father.

## 6. Swimming in a Current

Standing in chest-deep water, hold the child under the armpits in the horizontal position, facing you. Walking backward, create a *current* or *draft* of water with your body. Then let go of the child, who should be able to swim a short distance to you with the help of the current. Continue moving backwards throughout the entire activity. You will use a similar technique to teach the child to swim the width of the pool independently.

Father tells Noah, "Get ready to go under again," as father walks backwards.

Father continues to walk backwards, creating a current that helps Noah swim forward.

Father reaches for Noah.

Noah comes up for a breath.

## 7. Climbing Out of the Pool

Give your child frequent opportunity to climb *out* of the pool independently. This is important for safety. The steps leading out of the pool are the easiest way to exit the water. Give the child lots of opportunity to climb these stairs. At first provide some assistance for safety.

Also, give your child repeated opportunity to climb out of the pool from the side. The child may crawl out on the belly or creep on hands and knees, and eventually climb out and walk. Any or all methods are fine as long as they are done independently. Do this several times during each swimming session.

Do these activities in any order you choose. Each activity should be easy and fun. Remember, the child is learning how it feels from a sensory standpoint *and* is having the opportunity to express this information with newly acquired motor abilities.

Noah needs only a slight boost
to climb out of the pool.

The rest he does by himself.

He's off and walking.

## 8. Using a Ladder

Another important safety skill is the ability to climb up the pool ladder. Unfortunately some commercial pools only have ladders, not steps. This is why it is important to give the child lots of opportunity to swim to the ladder, hold onto it, and climb out.

Position yourself close enough to the ladder so the child can easily swim to it. After giving a gentle push toward the ladder, help the child grab onto the step or railing, stand, and climb up. Gradually, with less help from you, the child will become more independent. The objective is for the child to be totally independent at climbing out of the pool using a ladder. Repeat this several times during each session.

Your child can also learn to enter the water by climbing down

Father tells Noah not to move until he says, "OK."

Noah dives in.

He swims to father.

Well done.

the ladder. If your child is already able to swim from the concrete stairs, allow your child to sit on the ladder and swim to you.

## 9. Swim, Surface to Breathe, and Swim Again

Using the activities described previously, have your child swim toward you as you walk backwards. When necessary, help the child to the surface to breathe. Then ease your child back into the water to continue swimming towards you as you walk backwards.

Eventually, your child will be able to swim towards you, independently surface to breathe, then submerge, swim, and surface again. Encourage your child to do this frequently and for longer distances. Continue to walk backwards as your child repeats this sequence. Soon

Noah swims to father, who walks backwards.

Father reaches out for Noah.

Father brings Noah up for a breath.

Father repeats the process while continuing to walk backward.

Noah launches himself into the pool.

you and your child will realize how easy it can be to swim across the full width of the pool (about 6 yards or meters)! This will be a proud day, with great celebration for your child's huge accomplishment.

## 10. "Jumping" from a Sitting Position

While sitting on the edge of the pool, encourage your child to jump in and swim to you. It still may be necessary for your child to hold your finger while jumping in. As with the other activities, gradually encourage swimming farther to reach you. Eventually your child will be independently jumping into the water with great enthusiasm.

He swims to father.

Hugs and congratulations from father.

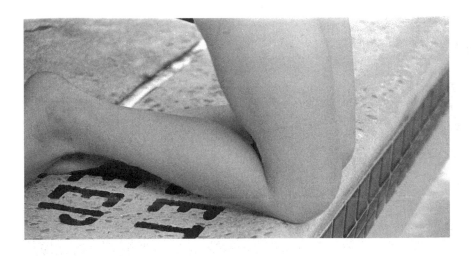

The knees should be an inch over the edge of the pool for a kneeling dive.

## 11. Diving from a Kneeling Position

For these next two activities, make sure the water is at least four feet deep but still standing depth for you. Be prepared to grab your child easily if necessary.

Have your child kneel on the edge of the pool facing you, kneeling with the knees slightly over the edge of the pool. The child extends the arms overhead and places one hand on top of the other. The child is asked to dive to you, not to the bottom of the pool. As the child leans over the edge of the pool and goes into the water, you should always be within reach.

It's important to teach the child to do a *shallow* dive toward you. You do not want him to dive toward the bottom of the pool!

## 12. Diving from a Standing Position

When your child can climb out of a regular pool independently and safely, it may be a good time to learn how to dive from a standing position.

*It's vital that your child understands these rules:*

- *Dive only with your permission.*

- *Dive only when the water is safely deep enough.*

- *Dive out, never toward the bottom.*

*Note: Always follow posted pool rules, including "no diving" areas.*

Marlowe, age eighteen months,
prepares to dive in.

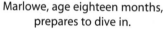

He then swims underwater.

Your child can stand with toes slightly over the edge of the pool
and feet slightly apart for balance. Slightly bend the knees and hold
the hands overhead, one on top of the other. Bending over the edge
of the pool, the child pushes with his knees and dives towards you.

When you repeat this activity, always let the child climb out of the
pool independently. This is a significant progression and requires calm
and patience. Always choose the part of the session when you are most
likely to receive the cooperation the activity requires. Your attitude
should be, "You have become a great swimmer and now you're ready
to learn to dive."

The final objective is for your child to dive into the pool independently, either from the sitting or standing position. Standing usually
makes the process easier because your child can launch farther into
the pool, and travel farther in the water.

The greater the speed entering the water in the horizontal position,
the easier it will be to maintain that position in the water. The child
proceeds to swim underwater, rise to the top to breathe, and continues
swimming. Initially you walk along offering assistance, but in time
the child completes this sequence independently.

Your child is now an independent swimmer!

Your child will want to do this over and over until you are too
tired to continue—and then he is too tired. Do not let this happen, as
the swimming session should end with victory, not fatigue.

## ADDITIONAL PLAYING AND FREE TIME

Once all the activities of a swimming session are completed with the appropriate repetition, give your child the opportunity to play and do the things he finds most enjoyable, whether diving, climbing the ladder, or combinations of these activities. Whatever the child wants to repeat is fine, *as long as you are always in the water.* On some days you or your child may be too tired to add this to the end of the session.

When the session is over and it's time to go home, have your child dry off with your help and return the towel to the bag. The goal is to leave happily and together.

Your child will achieve independence based upon consistent opportunity to swim. My oldest son, Marlowe, was a great swimmer at three months of age, but allergies exacerbated by the chemicals in the pool severely reduced his swimming opportunity. It took us an entire summer of swimming to bring him at nine months of age where he had been at three months. That was frustrating for all of us.

## PROGRESS AND FREQUENCY

At this point in the program it may be important to emphasize some key points for success based on frequency:

### Five Days or More of Swimming a Week

Excellent progress can be maintained when the child has the opportunity to swim five days a week or more. Under excellent conditions of weather and location, a child may be able to achieve the objective of swimming independently, as described above, before age two.

Not everyone lives in a suitable climate or has an indoor pool. With a less hospitable environment, it becomes increasingly more difficult to swim five days a week.

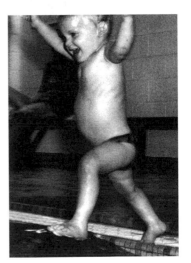

Kids love to jump into the water during playtime.

### Three Days or More of Swimming a Week

Good progress can be maintained when the child has the opportunity to swim three days a week or more. Here at The Institutes in Philadelphia, we have good conditions for swimming throughout the summer only. We maximize this opportunity and arrange for the children to swim five days a week or more during warm weather. Opportunity to swim gradually decreases in the fall and winter months. We are lucky to average two days a week of swimming at the local YMCA during this period. By mid-winter, the average may drop to one day a week.

## One Day or More of Swimming a Week

Progress may be maintained with two days a week of swimming, but it is our experience that when we are averaging one day a week of swimming during the winter, children can hold their own. In other words, they maintain the abilities they have but do not progress, or do so very slowly.

## Less Than One Day a Week of Swimming

It is difficult to progress with an average of less than one day a week of swimming. Any opportunity is better than none, but it is difficult to maintain an enthusiastic and enjoyable swimming program on less than one day a week.

No one knows better than the staff of The Institutes that mothers are extraordinary people. We do not doubt that some mothers could make progress in swimming even with little opportunity.

## Checklist for One- to Two-Year-Olds

- ☐ Frequent cuddling, with hugs and kisses.
- ☐ Bobbing up and down.
- ☐ Holding the side of the pool.
- ☐ Swimming to the steps.
- ☐ Floating on the back.
- ☐ Swimming from the steps to mother.
- ☐ Jumping and diving from a sitting position to mother. Progress to diving from a kneeling position, then from a standing position.
- ☐ Pushing off and swimming to mother.
- ☐ Swimming to mother and taking a breath, then submerging and continuing to swim.
- ☐ Climbing out of the pool; include using the ladder.

# 6

## Teaching Two- to Four-Year-Olds to Swim

The prerequisite for this program is that your child can happily and easily jump into the pool, swim across it (about 6 yards or meters), and climb out independently.

Some one-year-olds who are super swimmers are ready for the activities discussed in this chapter. Other children may be four years old or considerably older but have had little opportunity to swim, and so could be ready to start these activities now.

Children in this age group are extremely active physically, and they can be in constant motion. For this reason it continues to be essential for children to be well fed before swimming.

If your child is not already accustomed to wearing goggles, this is the time to introduce them. Using goggles has several advantages discussed previously in the chapter "Water Safety and Hygiene."

### LEARNING THE CRAWL STROKE

Ideally, by the age of four years a child swim can about 40 feet (or 12 meters) using the *crawl stroke*. This is a much more coordinated way of swimming. This will increase your child's speed and endurance and require less effort. It will also make the child a much more confident and independent swimmer.

Respiration continues to be a key to success. Turning the head to breathe is covered in detail in this chapter. Deeper, more controlled respiration is essential for learning to swim the crawl stroke independently.

Whenever we teach our children anything that is physical, intellectual, or social in nature, we carefully break the activity down into a step-by-step process. We do this because the sensory areas of the brain will receive and store information best if it is presented to the brain in a *precise, discrete,* and *unambiguous* way. The importance of presenting the brain with information this way is explained in detail in my father's books *How To Multiply Your Baby's Intelligence* and *How To Give Your Baby Encyclopedic Knowledge.* We use these same principles to teach babies reading, math, advanced gymnastics, and even to play the violin.

We do our utmost to emphasize only one step at a time. However, it may not always be practical. While learning to inhale, for example, it's difficult not to exhale. Despite this, we will try to *focus* and *emphasize* one key step at a time.

We have broken down the components of the crawl stroke in order to teach them easily and successfully. There are four basic components of the crawl stroke, some with two parts:

1.  Breathing (rotate the head and inhale, straighten the head and exhale)

2.  Using the arms

3.  Flutter kicking with the legs

4.  Keeping the body straight (streamlining)

Now we're ready to present to the brain—with great frequency, intensity, and duration—how it feels to do each of the crawl stroke components. Once this is accomplished, we will present the brain with two components together, then three components. Later we will present all the components simultaneously.

There are specific regions of the brain called the *integrative areas,* which combine and integrate information about vision, tactility, balance, and coordination. Teaching your child a new stroke actually grows and develops these areas of the brain. The better developed these areas, the more easily other new abilities can be acquired (such as speech).

The crawl stroke requires efficient breathing as well. As discussed previously, the better developed your child's respiration, the faster language will be developed and the better will be the child's overall state of health.

From the child's standpoint, the entire process is a joyous game of playing with you in the water. Games, joking, and laughing are all that is required for the child to enjoy what is happening. However, it's also important for you to briefly explain each activity to your child before performing it.

Below are the four basic components of the crawl stroke and how to teach them:

# 1. Breathing

This can be accomplished one of two ways. While the *emphasis* is on inhaling, the child will obviously have to exhale too.

## Inhaling While Holding the Edge of the Pool (Method A)

Your child faces the side of the pool in shallow water with arms fully extended and holds the edge with both hands. With the face in the water, the child turns the head to the side (in effect trying to touch chin to shoulder) and inhales. Then the child returns to face down in the water to exhale. Alternate evenly, turning to the left and right sides.

Begin by turning the head two to four times, gradually building up to ten times. The activity should be short and easy.

At first children may not be thrilled about repetitive activities. Provide congratulations and encouragement often. Don't hesitate to create a game to make it more enjoyable, such as singing a song, saying hello, or kissing the head as the child turns to inhale.

**Method A**

Veronica Vasquez, age three, helps teach her younger sister, Gabriella, age two, how to hold her head in the water facing the bottom.

Veronica rotates her head out of the water and inhales.

**Method B**

Noah, age four, swims as father briefly holds his head and walks backwards.

He gently rotates Noah's head out of the water and instructs
him to inhale as father continues to walk backwards.

After Noah inhales, father releases him and moves out of the way.

As the days pass, when you are convinced your child can easily turn and inhale independently, gradually reduce your help until the child is turning the head ten times. Providing your child is enjoying this, you may build up to doing this activity three times throughout the pool session.

Eventually hold your child's legs up so they are parallel to the bottom of the pool. Now the child is in a proper swimming position and the brain feels what it's like to be in this correct position *and* breathe.

## Inhaling While Swimming (Method B)

While you walk backwards the child swims toward you. Gently grasp the sides of your child's head between your hands and rotate it to the side. Do not cover the ears, as this can be annoying. Say "inhale" and "exhale" at the appropriate times. *Don't pull the child by the head.* Do this to both the right and left sides.

Continue until your child can perform the movements comfortably and independently. As in Method A, gradually build up to doing ten inhalations without stopping. Then increase to three sessions of ten inhalations. Praise your child frequently, and give kisses and hugs.

## Exhaling While Holding the Edge of the Pool (Method A)

Even though your child has already learned to exhale with the above activity, this part simply *emphasizes* the exhalation component of the crawl stroke.

Using the procedures from Method A to the right, have your child perform the same routine as when inhaling. But this time emphasize exhalation when the child's face is in the water.

Teach the child that to exhale into the water is exactly like blowing bubbles. The child may exhale only a small amount at first, but encourage this initial success. The goal is for the child to turn the head and inhale, then turn back (so the child is face down) and exhale into the water.

Repeat this ten times nonstop. Work up to doing three sessions of ten times nonstop. Give the child opportunity to alternate inhaling to the left and right sides during head turning. This is to avoid the habit of only rotating to one side.

In time, hold your child's legs parallel to the bottom of the pool. This is important for your child to feel how it feels to breathe and swim in a horizontal position.

**Method A**

Veronica shows Gabriella how to exhale into the water. Note the bubbles around her head.

Gabriella copies her sister and exhales into the water.

Gabriella starts to rotate her face out of the water.

### *Exhaling While Swimming (Method B)*

Using Method B, have your child swim and emphasize exhaling into the water. As necessary, help rotate the chin out of the water. Gradually build to swimming with ten exhalations into the water, and eventually add two more sessions of ten.

**Method B**

Winston Zeberlein, age four, exhales underwater as he swims towards mother.

Mother holds Winston's head and helps him turn it to inhale. His body remains horizontal and in motion.

## 2. Using the Arms

In this activity, you will help your child: a) pick one arm out of the water, b) extend it above the head, c) put it back in the water, and d) pull it through the water.

### *While Holding Child (Method A)*

Stand in shallow water with your feet apart in a stable stance. With one arm, hold the child straight and horizontal in the water against your hip. With your other hand help the child lift one arm out of the water, extend it overhead, reach, put it in the water, and pull in the direction of head to toe. This last motion pulls the child through the water. The hands should be open with fingers together.

Do this ten times with the left arm, then ten times with the right. Over a week, increase to three opportunities during the session. Continue to guide as necessary and soon your child will be doing the movements accurately and independently.

**Method A**

Holding Winston around the waist, mother helps move his left arm into the water.

Mother helps pull his arm through the water. They do this many times.

Mother switches Winston to her left side.

She repeats the process with his right arm.

## *While Child Stands (Method B)*

If your child is too large, or if you are too small, there may be a more comfortable method. Your child can stand in shallow water with feet apart, bending slightly at the waist. Stand behind your child holding the waist. Assist as above, first one arm ten times, then the other.

When your child can do these movements independently, begin to alternate arms. Stroke with the left and then the right. Gradually build up to one session of twenty strokes (ten strokes for each arm). With time, do three separate sessions of twenty strokes.

**Method B**

Mother raises Winston's right arm and moves it toward the water.

She pulls Winston's arm straight down through the water to his waist.

Mother repeats the process with his left arm. Winston feels what it's like to pull his arm through the water.

His right arm comes out of the water to repeat the cycle.

## 3. Flutter Kicking

### *While Holding the Side of the Pool (Method A)*

The child holds the side of the pool and kicks. The flutter kick consists of keeping the knees relatively straight and moving the whole leg from the hips. The distance the foot travels is short and the kicking movement is fast. The purpose is to help keep the body horizontal in the water and to propel the body forward.

The child kicks with one leg ten times, and then switches to the other. In the course of a swimming session, gradually build up to three sessions of ten kicks with each leg. When the quality of kicking is rhythmic and coordinated, the child can begin kicking with both legs. Gradually build up to a total of twenty kicks nonstop. Finally do this for all three of the opportunities during a swimming session.

### *While Holding Child (Method B)*

When your child is kicking with both legs, perform the same activity farther out in the pool. Hold your child with both hands under the belly so you support some of the child's weight. Increase to three sessions of twenty kicks during the swim.

Winston flutter kicks independently as his mother hold him in the middle of the pool.

**Method A**

Father tries to keep the water out of his eyes while he holds Noah's left leg. He flutter kicks with his right leg.

Father holds Noah's right leg while Noah flutter kicks with his left leg.

Noah flutter kicks independently with both legs.

**Method B**

Winston prepares to dive into
the pool from the sitting position.

## 4. Keeping the Body Straight (Streamlining)

This important body posture—streamlining—can help isolate the components of swimming. The child streamlines the body by making it straight, which allows it to move more easily through the water. Arms are straight ahead, one open hand on top of the other. The body is straight, from the tips of the fingers to the feet.

Begin by having the child sit on the edge of the pool or on the pool steps. In a diving position (leaning forward with arms overhead) the child dives into the water, pushing off the side or steps, and straightens the whole body. Facing down in the water, the child flutter kicks to you while maintaining the streamline position. This is a tremendous achievement, so enjoy many hugs and kisses.

Build up to doing this activity at least three times during the swim. With improvement, encourage longer distances without breathing. Longer duration helps the brain learn how it feels to streamline more effectively. Better breath holding further improves respiration.

Winston leans over, ready to fall
forward and push off with his feet.

Winston remains straight and horizontal as he flutter kicks.
Mother walks backwards as Winston swims forward.

With further improvement, have the child take a quick break to breathe, then continue to flutter kick while breath holding. Your child should also stay streamlined during the pause to breathe. The young swimmer can best do this by rotating the head toward the shoulder that is above the surface. Then the child can inhale. Encourage your child to comfortably hold his breath for longer periods in order to travel farther. The goal is to easily swim the entire width of the pool (about 6 yards or meters) with the minimum number of breaths.

| Winston pushes off the pool steps and streamlines to mother. | Mother moves backwards as Winston approaches. | Mother gets ready to congratulate Winston. |

**Method A**

Winston exhales into the water
while flutter kicking.

As he kicks, Winston raises his head
to inhale and continues the cycle.

**Method B**

Winston exhales into the water and
continues to flutter kick, as his mother
holds him in the middle of the pool.

## COMBINING THE COMPONENTS OF THE CRAWL STROKE

Now your child's brain has learned each component of the crawl stroke and can automatically duplicate each without great difficulty. Now the brain can combine each component in a logical step-by-step manner.

## 1. Combine Breathing and Kicking

There are three ways this can be accomplished. Perform one, two, or all three.

### Holding the Edge of the Pool (Method A)

While the child is kicking, help him simultaneously turn the head and inhale, ending with an exhale into the water. Perhaps the child turns to breathe once every six kicks or so, and will gradually become more coordinated and simultaneously kick and breathe. Do this activity of rotating the head and breathing while kicking twenty times. Build up to doing this three times during a swim.

Gradually reduce your assistance as your child becomes more independent.

### Holding the Child in the Middle of the Pool (Method B)

Holding under the belly or by the hips, instruct the child to start kicking, and then rotate the head to inhale and exhale. Gradually increase the activity to twenty kicks with inhalation and exhalation as required. Do this at least three times during each swim.

While flutter kicking, Winston rotates
his head to take a breath with mother's help.

## Mother Helps Turn the Head as the Child Streamlines (Method C)

We have already begun this process with streamlining. The child dives into the pool from the sitting position and streamlines across the pool, as described previously. Gently assist turning the child's head to the side. Simultaneously, say "inhale" and "exhale" appropriately. The first objective is for the child to breathe this way while streamlining the width of the pool. Eventually your child will be able to perform this activity independently.

**Method C**

Winston pushes off from the steps in the streamline position—arms are straight and hands are clasped.

Walking backwards, mother helps Winston rotate his head to inhale. Winston then continues to kick and streamline forward.

## 2. Combine Breathing, Kicking, and Using the Arms

Your child is now ready to perform the crawl stroke independently, which incorporates breathing, kicking, and using the arms. Providing the individual activities were successful, it will be relatively easy to put it all together.

Your child dives into the water from a sitting position, pushes off the side, and streamlines across the pool while breathing and kicking correctly, as described previously. Now add the arm movement. The head is turned to take a breath as the arm on that side is extended overhead and forward.

Walk alongside your child in case assistance is needed. Simply touching a limb may be enough to remind your child how to use it properly. When you begin this activity, it is important to start by diving in. This gives your child the momentum to keep his body streamlined and horizontal. Encouragement, hugs, and kisses are very important at this stage.

With each trip across the pool, your child will gradually improve. Build up to ten trips across the pool. Your child can now perform an independent crawl stroke. Speed will eventually improve as your child learns to remain in the horizontal position.

As your child progresses to this level of swimming, there are two specific techniques to watch in order to help your child improve.

• Optimal arm movement is very important. The crawl stroke may create fatigue because children can have difficulty pulling their arms completely out of the water. The arm muscles in young children are not well developed, but these activities will strengthen the arms, thus making the crawl stroke easier.

• The second greatest difficulty for children is doing a true flutter kick. They tend to kick from the knees, which creates a slower kick and more fatigue. Ideally the feet should be just below the water line. If they are coming out of the water the knees are bending too much. With more fatigue the child kicks more slowly and the body begins to drop into a diagonal position, making swimming increasingly more difficult. Encourage your child to keep the knees straight and move from the hips with short, fast kicks.

## 3. Breathing to Both Sides

When little children become independent at the crawl stroke, they often lock themselves into the habit of breathing only to one side. Right-handed people usually find it easier to breathe to the right, and left-handed people to the left.

Before they get into the habit of breathing only to one side, it is important to teach children to breathe to both sides when swimming the crawl stroke. This is called *alternate* breathing. The child breathes to the right side, then to the left side, then to the right side, and so on. There are three ways we can establish this good habit.

### *Holding the Side of the Pool (Method A)*

When the child is holding the edge of the pool and practicing inhaling and exhaling into the water, give the child the opportunity to breathe to the right several times until he is good at it. Then give him the opportunity to breathe to the left several times until it is done well. Finally, combine the two so the child inhales to the right, exhales into the water, inhales to the left, exhales into the water, inhales to the right, etc.

### *While Holding Child (Method B)*

When you are holding the child in the middle of the pool and practicing inhaling and exhaling into the water, as explained earlier, have him breathe to the right many times, and then to the left many times, until they are both learned. Eventually, combine the two until he is successfully performing alternate breathing.

### *While Swimming (Method C)*

When your child is doing the crawl stroke, gently hold his head and help him breathe to the right side until he is good at it. Then help him practice breathing to the left side until it is second nature. Finally, help your child turn his head to breathe, alternating to the right side and the left side. Concentrate on breathing to both sides until it is habitual.

When the child wants to swim very fast, he will probably find it easier to breathe only to one side. However, a goal of this book is for children to find endurance swimming enjoyable. It is greatly pre-

Mason, age two, Noah, age three, and Winston, age four, use their goggles to play on the bottom of the pool and retrieve rings and toys.

ferred in endurance swimming for children to have the habit of breathing alternately to the right and the left. Physically this helps create well-balanced bodies, equally strong on the right and left sides.

## PLAYTIME

Always begin your swimming lesson when you and your child first get into the water. Like babies, two- to four-year-olds learn best when they are well rested and fed, and do not need to go to the toilet. Also, it is best to teach children *before* they are tired from play. It is much harder to stop them and then begin a high-quality teaching session.

Give your child the opportunity to play in the water after each lesson. Play is an integral part of the child's swimming experience, and children are experts at creating their own games. This provides opportunity to swim underwater and adds confidence and independence.

Children love toys such as rings and brightly colored objects that are easy to spot underwater. These toys will help them play for longer periods. Children enjoy riding on your back as you swim, and love to race and chase you and other children. I have seen the game "Marco Polo" played around the world in many languages. When my children were little enough, they loved holding themselves in the "tuck" position (holding knees tightly against the chest), and letting me throw them into the air. They would splash into the water and then swim back to me, until I was too tired to throw them anymore.

Mason plays with mother. Mother dives underwater and Mason goes for a ride! Parents and children invent all types of games.

## THE FINAL GOAL

When a child can swim many *widths* of the pool, progress to swimming the *length*. The final goal is for your child to dive in from one end of the pool, swim the entire length (12 yards or 12 meters) using the crawl stroke, and climb out. You may need to swim alongside your child as he progresses from swimming half the length, to three-

Noah, age four, prepares to dive into the pool and swim the length.

He dives in!

Doing the crawl stroke, he turns his head to the side and inhales.

quarters, to the entire length. Eventually, with great fanfare, your child will accomplish this goal.

With this success, prepare and frame a special certificate for your child: *INDEPENDENT SWIMMER OF THE CRAWL STROKE* with your child's name and the date (see Appendix, page 109). You have both earned it!

His body is straight and parallel to the bottom of the pool while he flutter kicks.

Nearing the wall, his left arm reaches forward to pull himself through the water.

He completes the length and climbs out.

# Checklist for Two- to Four-Year-Olds

☐ Frequent cuddling, with hugs and kisses.

☐ Breathing and head turning while holding the side of the pool: rotate the chin towards the shoulder and inhale, straighten the head as it enters the water and exhale (Method A).

☐ Performing the same activity as above, but now hold your child in the middle of the pool (Method B).

☐ Using arms for the crawl stroke. Begin by holding the child on your side and progress to independent swimming (Method C).

☐ Flutter kicking as the child holds the side of the pool.

☐ Flutter kicking as you hold the child on the side of your body.

☐ Diving in and streamlining to you from the side of the pool.

☐ Streamlining and flutter kicking.

☐ Combine streamlining, kicking, and breathing.

☐ Add pulling with the arms so the child can do the complete stroke.

☐ Diving into the water from the standing position and streamlining.

☐ From in the water, dive safely to the bottom and retrieve an object. Start in shallow water and gradually move to deeper water.

☐ Dive in safely, swim the entire length (about 12 yards or 12 meters) using the crawl stroke, and climb out, all independently.

# 7

## Teaching Four- to Six-Year-Olds to Swim

The prerequisite for this program is that your child enthusiastically dives into the pool, swims the entire length (about 12 yards or 12 meters) using the crawl stroke, and easily climbs out.

Provided your child has learned the activities in the previous chapters, all that remains is to improve the *quality* of the crawl stroke through frequent swimming. As this occurs, it becomes easier to swim, speed increases, and the child feels more secure and safer in the water.

In the event that your child is older and has already learned the crawl stroke but you would like to improve the quality, we advise combining all the information in the previous chapter with this one.

From age four to six we concentrate on four key areas:

1. Improving the quality of streamlining

2. Improving endurance

3. Improving the quality of the crawl stroke *outside* the pool

4. Improving the quality of diving

### 1. Improving Streamlining and the Crawl Stroke

A. Streamlining

Improving streamlining will improve the quality of your child's crawl stroke. Children whose stroke is more efficient can swim much farther with less effort.

By now your child is accomplished at streamlining at least the width of a typical private pool (about 6 yards or 6 meters).

Gradually increase the number of times your child streamlines the width of the pool. Build up to five widths in each swimming lesson, then build up to ten widths. Make sure the child keeps his body straight. One open hand is on top of the other, arms are straight, and legs are straight and flutter kicking. The child should hold his breath and breathe when necessary. Continue to work on holding the breath longer, keeping the entire body straight, and taking the minimum number of breaths.

B. Crawl Stroke

*Four-Year-Olds:* The objective for the four-year-old is to increase gradually to swimming the *width* of a pool at least 15 times (± 100 yards or meters) in a swim session. Encourage a straight body, good-quality flutter kicking and arm motion, and coordinated breathing. Swimming these widths should be spread throughout the session. Eventually provide your child the opportunity to increase the nonstop swimming ability by building up to the entire 15 widths nonstop. This is a gradual process that occurs over an entire year.

*Five-Year-Olds:* Gradually increase from swimming 15 widths to 15 *lengths* (± 200 yards or meters) in a swim session. Swimming these lengths (± 12 yards or meters each) should be spread throughout the entire session. Sometimes the child should swim an entire *lap* (± 24 yards or meters) nonstop. When your child can easily swim four laps, gradually increase the nonstop distance until your child can easily swim 200 yards or meters.

*Six-Year-Olds:* Gradually build up (over a six-month period) from roughly eight laps of a pool to 16 laps (± 400 yards or meters) in the course of a swimming session. When your child does this consistently, begin to increase the nonstop distance until your child can swim 400 yards or meters nonstop.

## 2. Improving Endurance

Improving the child's endurance refers to increasing the function of the *aerobic system*, which comprises the heart, lungs, and aerobic muscles. While *aerobic* refers to the use of oxygen, it also means the child will burn more fat to obtain energy. Science has well established the importance of aerobic activity and its importance to optimal health.

Most importantly aerobic activity improves the oxygenation of the brain, which is necessary for its growth and development. Aerobic also relates to the intensity of the activity; in this case aerobic

Ariel de Ment is a typical aerobic swimmer of the International School. At six years of age she can swim 400 meters (¼ mile) nonstop in ten minutes. She pulls her left arm through the water, inhales, and begins to pull her right arm out of the water.

Ariel continues to flutter kick while bringing her right arm forward.

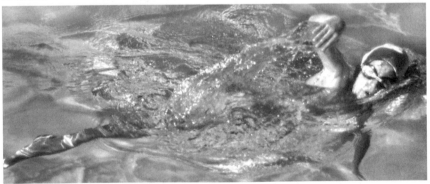

Ariel can swim more than 600 meters nonstop.

She exhales into the water as the next stroke begins.

means relatively easy, which is the best way to improve endurance and health.

*Anaerobic* refers to reduced oxygen, which occurs during harder workouts of short distances, such as an all-out sprint. This is not appropriate for young children learning how to swim. If a child is swimming anaerobically, it will be a more difficult and uncomfortable session.

Activities such as running, biking, cross-country skiing, and others also require endurance. By developing good aerobic function through swimming, it will be easier to improve endurance with any physical activity.

We have three years, from the child's fourth birthday through his sixth year, to increase the total distance and improve endurance. Thus it is a slow, gentle process. Ideally your child should hardly realize that he is swimming longer distances.

Technically speaking, a proper aerobic program requires physical activity that causes a rise in heart rate that increases circulation to all the organs and glands. Swimming must be maintained for a period of 15 to 20 minutes in order to obtain aerobic benefits. For more information about the whys and hows of an aerobic program for your entire family, read *In Fitness and In Health* by Dr. Philip Maffetone.

## 3. Improving the Quality of the Crawl Stroke *Outside* the Pool

These activities are extremely convenient and can be done anywhere you have a bench. Although not ideal, they could even be done on a bed or floor. This opportunity to "swim" even though there is no pool can reinforce everything your child is learning in the water.

These are all components of the crawl stroke with which the child is totally familiar. There is nothing new here except that the activities are done on land.

You can physically help the child as needed, just as in the water, and gradually reduce your help as your child improves.

### *Breathing*

Have your child lie face down on a bench with the head extended off the end of it. The bench can be cushioned. The body should be fully supported by the bench. Your child turns the head and inhales, then straightens the head and exhales exactly as in the water. Gradually your child should increase alternating inhaling to the left and then

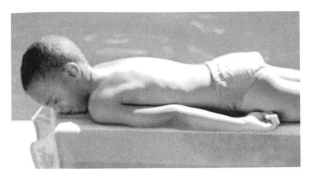

Joshua Allman, age four, lies prone on the bench. He faces the ground and exhales.

He rotates his chin to his shoulder and inhales

inhaling to the right. The objective is to increase alternate breathing until it becomes a habit.

## Flutter Kicking

This is another good way to teach your child to keep the knees straight and to kick from the hips. Have your child lie on the bench so the upper thighs and legs extend past the bench and are parallel to the floor.

Jake Marrazzo, age five, flutter kicks on the bench.

Mother holds a bucket over Jake's feet as he flutter kicks. The leg movements come from his hips, not his knees.

Jake raises his right arm to place it in "the water" and pull.
His left arm is down and straight.

As left hand enters the water, his right arm is down and straight.

With the legs held straight, your child makes short fluttering kicks. You can use a ring or place your hands above and below the feet to teach your child to keep the kick short and fast.

## Pulling with the Arms

Have your child lie on the bench with the head extended off the end of it. The bench needs to be narrow enough that both arms are free to rotate as in swimming. Teach your child to raise each arm overhead and extend it fully before pulling it back. When your child does this well, combine pulling with the arms and breathing.

The ideal moment for inhaling is when the hand is exiting the water. When your child's head rotates to the left for an inhalation, the left hand should be exiting the water as the child inhales. The left arm then is pulled forward as the head rotates into the water. Also, practice inhaling to the right side. Finally, practice alternate breathing to the right and then the left. Do this on the bench and in the water.

As the hand enters the water, the fingers need to be relaxed. The fingers may be held together or slightly apart. Practice this in and out of the water.

Jake prepares to pull with his left arm while flutter kicking.

Jake pulls with his right arm while kicking.

## Combining Pulling with Arms and Flutter Kicking

Providing your child has sufficiently practiced flutter kicking and pulling with the arms, the next step is to combine the two activities. At first, help your child move his legs while the child moves his arms. Gradually reduce your assistance with the feet until the child can independently move his arms correctly while flutter kicking.

### Combining Pulling with Arms, Flutter Kicking, and Breathing

Start this activity only after all other movements are learned. Begin with the first activity, pulling with the arms. When it is going well, add flutter kicking, and then breathing. Have your child alternate breathing to the left and then immediately to the right.

Initially, limit these activities (listed to the right) to about fifteen seconds each. Gradually, over a few months, build up the duration of each activity to one minute. When your child has achieved one minute for each of the five activities, you have reached the limit for a four-year-old. Spread the activities throughout the day. Keep it easy and fun.

For a five-year-old, gradually increase to doing one minute of each activity twice a day. The ten one-minute sessions should be divided throughout the day so they are short and easy to accomplish.

**Five Activities for Outside the Pool to Improve the Crawl Stroke**

1. Breathing
2. Flutter Kicking
3. Pulling with the Arms
4. Combining Pulling with Arms and Flutter Kicking
5. Combining Pulling with Arms, Flutter Kicking, and Breathing

Joshua combines all of the activities. He pulls with his left arm as he breathes to the right side.

He flutter kicks with his legs and strokes with his arms.

Jake kneels with his knees overhanging the edge of the pool. His hands are clasped and his arms are straight.

Jake leans forward with his arms overhead.

He does a shallow dive.

For a six-year-old, gradually build up to doing each of the five activities three times, spread throughout the day. The total time is 15 minutes a day.

Do these activities on the days you cannot go to the pool.

## 4. Improving the Quality of Diving

We continue to work on improving diving from the ages of four to six. However, as your child grows larger, you must be increasingly more conscientious about diving safety, adhering to all regulations of public pools. For private pools, you must be very conservative and only permit your child to dive in your presence and in water deep enough so that there is no possibility your child could hit the bottom.

The three options for diving remain the same:

### *Sitting*

The child sits on the side of the pool, leans forward, fully extends the arms with one hand over the other, and then dives in.

### *Kneeling*

The child kneels on the side of the pool with the torso erect and knees slightly over the edge, leans forward, fully extends arms with one hand over the other, and dives in.

### *Standing*

The child stands with toes slightly over the edge of the pool and knees slightly bent. He then leans forward, fully extends arms with one hand over the other, pushes forward, and dives in. Teach the child to dive parallel to the surface of the water, heading slightly downward so as not to belly-flop.

Encourage the child to stay straight by diving through a ring (such as a hula-hoop).

Children love to dive. Sprinkle frequent opportunities to dive throughout your swimming sessions.

## MAKE SWIMMING LONGER DISTANCES FUN

The following will help your child enjoy swimming longer distances:

- Continue to focus on streamlining to improve body position.

- Use the activities that can be done *outside* the pool to improve quality.

- Gradually build up the quantity of swimming in one session.

- When your child has reached the desired quantity of swimming, gradually increase the nonstop swimming distance.

- Swim consistently.

- Make sure your child inhales to the left and then to the right.

- Continue to use your imagination to make the entire process fun. Ultimately, swimming *with* your child will make it more enjoyable for both of you. You can play games of tag, or race for fun, giving your child a "head start." Older children, relatives, or friends can play the same kinds of games with your child.

**Goals:**

- Four-year-olds: Gradually build up to 100 meters nonstop of the crawl stroke.

- Five-year-olds: Gradually build up to 200 meters nonstop of the crawl stroke.

- Six-year-olds: Gradually build up to 400 meters nonstop of the crawl stroke.

## A NOTE ABOUT OTHER STROKES

Providing that your child loves to swim and is doing very well with all aspects of the crawl stroke, there is absolutely no reason not to begin teaching other strokes. These strokes go beyond the scope of this book. The key is to continue to teach your child in a loving way. Break down all activities into a step-by-step process. Your child needs to win in one activity and then go on to the next. Begin with short sessions and gradually increase the frequency. Begin by assisting your child and then work towards independence.

## BACK CRAWL

Ariel extends her left arm straight out of the water.

She pulls through the water with her right arm.

She flutter kicks, as in the crawl stroke.

She repeats the process.

# Checklist for Four- to Six-Year-Olds

☐ Frequent cuddling with hugs and kisses.

☐ Streamlining with independent breathing and flutter kicking.

☐ Performing crawl stroke, gradually increasing the total distance of nonstop swimming. Have your child inhale to the left, and then to the right.

☐ Improve diving in the sitting position, kneeling position, and standing position.

☐ Four-year-olds: Gradually build up to 100 yards or meters of nonstop swimming

☐ Five-year-olds: Gradually build up to 200 yards or meters of nonstop swimming.

☐ Six-year-olds: Gradually build up to 400 yards or meters of nonstop swimming.

☐ For advanced swimming, learn other strokes and flip turns.

## For those performing bench activities (face down)

☐ Practice rotating the chin to the shoulder and inhale, then straighten the head and exhale.

☐ Flutter kicking: knees should be over the end of the bench and movement is from the hips, not the knees.

☐ Rotate and pull with both arms: arms should move over and below the sides of the bench.

☐ Combine pulling with arms and flutter kicking.

☐ Combine pulling with arms, flutter kicking and breathing.

# Activities Checklist
# for All Ages

☐ Retrieve rings and other toys from bottom of pool.

☐ Swim between the legs of one parent,
then both parents.

☐ Ride on a parent's back, like riding a dolphin.

☐ While standing in deep water, a parent throws the
child into the water.

☐ Race for fun.

☐ Play tag.

☐ Push off the bottom and rocket to the surface.

☐ See how far your child can swim underwater.

☐ Swim in deep water.

☐ Play soccer with goals at each end of the pool.

☐ Go underwater and somersault forward.

☐ Go underwater and somersault backwards.

☐ Stand on your hands on the bottom of the pool.

☐ Play Marco Polo.

☐ Play basketball with a floating net.

☐ Play water polo.

☐ Invent your own activities.

# 8

## *Swimming and Physical Excellence*

**B**abies love to swim and should have the opportunity from birth because it helps stimulate and develop optimal brain function. Virtually all the muscles are used to some degree when swimming, so this activity also provides an excellent aerobic workout. In short, swimming can be an important part of a healthy lifestyle that benefits your child for life.

Children who are competent and confident swimmers are more likely to confront new physical opportunities throughout life. Our hope is for them to be *participants* in life, not spectators.

Our definition of *Physical Excellence* includes being able to solve any physical problem encountered during life. This may include saving one's own life, or saving someone else's. Physical Excellence should also help children expand their intellectual and social horizons.

At The Institutes, our formula is:

*Physical Excellence = The Ideal Environment + Maximum Opportunity*

Successful swimming at all levels depends upon your ability to find the *ideal environment* in which the baby can swim. In the beginning this may mean a large bathtub, progressing to a larger pool and/or open water as appropriate. Success in swimming at all levels depends upon providing the *maximum opportunity* to swim. At least three days a week is recommended to maintain a good rate of progress. Excellent progress is achieved by five or more days a week.

It is also important to emphasize two important situations to *avoid:*

1. Never put your baby in a swimming program where you are not allowed to be present. The basis of any program should be to teach mother and child to continue the program independently.

2. We do not use or recommend flotation devices for teaching babies to swim. They prevent the brain from receiving real information about the water environment. Flotation devices create an *artificial* environment. The baby's brain only receives information about breathing, balance, coordination, tactility, etc., based upon the influence of a flotation device. If the baby then falls into the water without the flotation device, the consequences can be grave. Babies easily become *dependent* upon these devices and often can't function without them. Our objective is to develop *independent* swimmers. Of course we use life jackets when boating and when it is appropriate for water safety.

Reaching the goals outlined in this book can result in a child who is a great swimmer. Most competitive swim coaches would love to get their hands on such a child, but this comes with potential risks. Over-training, a no-pain, no-gain attitude, and other unhealthy approaches common in competitive sports have ruined many young athletes. Competition and team sports can be very healthy, but it's important for you to watch how your child is treated in these environments.

In addition, some children don't enjoy these activities. A child forced to play competitively is destined to fail, regardless of his or her swimming ability. This book is about giving children options so *they* can choose what they want. Self-determination is a key to success. If your child wants to join a swim team, find a caring coach who will encourage your child's love of swimming.

The opportunities and locations to swim on our planet are enormous, from a newborn swimming in a bath, to an older child swimming in a pool, stream, lake, sea, or ocean.

There is a world of activities and sports dependent upon water. People who love the water and are excellent swimmers have all these options available to them: lifesaving, boating, canoeing, kayaking, whitewater rafting, and sailing, to name a few. Sports such as surfing, wind surfing, snorkeling, and scuba diving all require the ability to swim.

As you apply the information in this book, the number of options you can give your child begins to multiply. The better the environment, the more opportunity and the more options are available. We carry the future of our children, grandchildren, and great grandchildren on our ability to be parents and to teach. Learning to swim early in life is one of the greatest gifts we can give a child.

# Acknowledgments

This book is very much a result of what I have learned during my entire life. It is based upon the work of my father and the staff of The Institutes for the Achievement of Human Potential. The Institutes work is based upon the life work of Dr. Temple Fay, who held both the chair of neurosurgery and neurology at Temple University Medical School in the 1950s.

My first memory of Dr. Fay is from when I was a five-year-old. I remember looking up at him in a hallway of The Institutes and thinking that this is the man who commands my father! My father was an infantry rifle company commander during the Second World War, and decorated for heroism by four nations. It was hard for me to imagine anyone who ordered my father around, but I had seen Dr. Fay do it. I figured he must be some kind of a god.

My mother and father raised me on the grounds of The Institutes, and I fell in love with their work as a child. This book is dedicated to them. They have always been a team. As a child I knew the most important goal in my life was to find a wife who would share with me the kind of relationship my parents have.

I found her in 1974 when she began her training as a staff member at The Institutes. Rosalind Klein Doman has been my best critic and companion since then, and we have been parents since 1983. Rosalind and I have also been professional colleagues. For more than 25 years, Rosalind has directed the baby swimming program at The Institutes. Her advice and input about swimming have been invaluable to me. She is also the associate director of The Institutes for the Achievement of Physical Excellence.

My sister, Janet, has been an important teacher in my life. She is currently the director of The Institutes.

As this book is about teaching, all the important teachers who taught me about good in teaching must be mentioned—John McIlvaine, Dan Charles, and Professor John Fout at Bard College.

Great teachers who taught me at The Institutes were: Dr. Edward LeWinn, Dr. Evan Thomas, Dr. Raymundo Veras, Dr. Neil Harvey, and Dr. Roselise Wilkinson.

My first experience teaching babies to swim was in 1975. The Institutes sent me to Japan to teach English to Japanese mothers so they could teach their tiny children. After working at the Early Development Association in Tokyo, I went to Melbourne, Australia. There I had the pleasure of watching Tim and Claire Timmermans. The Timmermans family had immigrated to Australia from the Netherlands. They were swimming coaches who taught their babies how to swim.

In the Timmerman's pool I saw Claire lovingly teach babies in the water. Any baby that was crying would be handed to Claire. Almost immediately the baby would relax and settle down.

When I returned home, as part of my responsibilities for the mobility development for both brain-injured and well children, I began to teach the mothers of brain-injured children. Our object was to teach their children to move in water and to swim. Shortly thereafter we opened the Evan Thomas Institute and started teaching mothers to teach their well babies. I began that swimming program.

In 1986, we had the pleasure of working with Igor Tcharkovski in Moscow. He is the pioneer of baby swimming in Russia and taught us the use of the shower to develop breath holding.

My dear friends and colleagues at The Institutes have helped make this book a reality. They include: Susan Aisen, director of Intellectual Excellence; Ann Ball, director of Physiological Excellence; the vice directors of The Institutes, Teruki Uemura, Miki Nakayachi, and Dr. Ernesto Vasquez; and the staff members of these Institutes, Dr. Lee Wong, Kathy Myers, Eliane Hollanda, Susanna Horn, and Dr. Diana Martinez.

As the director emeritus of The Institute for the Achievement of Physical Excellence I have been a part of "a band of brothers" and sisters. This group includes: Leia Coelho Reilly, the current director of this Institute; past director Bruce Hagy; vice director Rumiko Ion Doman, my niece; assistant director Nati Tenacio Myers; coordinator

Jennifer Canepa; senior staff member Rogelio Marty; and Susan Cameron, staff member and special friend of my family. Our applied kinesiology biofeedback team of Dr. Carl Weisse and Dr. Leon Morales are an important part of this team.

The medical staff has contributed to this book as well. Dr. Cora-lee Thompson, our medical director, has also taught her two boys to be wonderful swimmers. Dr. Leland Green and Dr. Denise Malkowitz helped me through some difficult periods of my own health.

Dr. Ralph Pelligra, chairman of the Medical Institutional Review Board, and his wife, Olivia Fernandez Pelligra, a director, are essential members of the team. Dr. Mihai Dimancescu, chairman of The Institutes board of directors and our neurosurgeon, contributed by answering my questions about the brain.

All of the above have dedicated their lives to the children and their parents. They have agonized over the problems of our profoundly brain-injured children and they have resolved to find the solutions to their problems. They have rejoiced over the victories of both the hurt and well children. They have done it all with love and the milk of human kindness.

The clinical and medical staff could not do their jobs without the support of the administrative staff headed by Linda Maletta and the finance staff directed by Robert Derr. They include: Brian Bradley, Jill Bell, Connie Breyer, Dorothy Coulston, Emma Del Rosario, Philomena Fishbourne, Neal Gauger, Shirley Hollis, Nest Holvey, Milan Hurtak, Van Ingram, Jim Kaliss, Julian Meyer, Alan Myers, Chip Myers, Harriet Pinsker, Dawn Price, Juaneta Richards, Gloria Rittenhouse, Judy Reif, David Rush, Jerry Schwartz, Eve Selya, Dolores Simonetta, Mary Standley, Dan Walker, Marsha Walsh, and B. White.

The preparation of the manuscript and the more than two thousand photographs and slides was the collaboration by the assistants to directors. The executive secretary, my own Aunt Cathy Ruhling, and Tammy Cadden, assistant to the director, supported my own staff. Kathie Knell ignored my bad moods and encouraged the good ones to get the work done. It was she who prepared edit after edit over a period of five years!

The Institutes editor, Janet Gauger, edited the book and prepared it for publication. By good fortune she is also our swimming coach. She taught her own two babies to be superb swimmers, lifeguards, and swimming instructors. Our editorial assistant, Lori O'Connor, helped in preparing the book.

The unsung hero of this book is Dr. Philip Maffetone, who writes beautifully and loves doing it. His books and professional articles are published around the world. He also edited the book and helped it to be published on time.

Christmas has always been a very special occasion for our family. My first memory of Sherman Hines came the Christmas after he and his wife, Andrea, attended the *How To Multiply Your Baby's Intelligence* Course in 1980. Sherman sent my father a copy of his beautiful book of photographs of the Canadian province of Alberta. After we raved about the book, we saw he had dedicated it to my father! Who can ever top a present like that? Well, only Sherman Hines. The photographer laureate of The Institutes, Sherman Hines, produced the majority of the photography in this book.

Jim Kaliss, David Kerper, and Dr. Jerry Morantz, a personal friend and member of our Institutional Review Board, contributed photographs as well. Jim Kaliss painstakingly scanned and prepared all of the photographs for printing.

The staff of The Institutes, Europe, who I have the joy of directing, are a part of my Italian family. The Institutes is located in the beautiful countryside of Pisa, in Tuscany. My Italian sister, Marcella Serafin, and my brother, Fulvio Pompei, work with our staff of Graziana Ceccanti, Lucia Giorgi, Mara Rossi, and our extraordinary chef, Marisa Bocelli. Member of our board of directors, Philip Phillips, and teacher extraordinaire, Diane Phillips, hold a special place in my heart. Dr. Carlo Valenti is a board member and his wife, Dr. Elisabetta Di Pangrazio, is our medical consultant in Europe.

Lastly, I wish to thank the four beings who taught me the most about babies swimming: Marlowe Lemle Doman, Spencer Stevenson Doman, Morgan Paolina Doman, and Noah Glenn Doman.

# *Appendix*

## BABY SWIMMING PRODUCTS

In most cases the products below can be found at your local hardware or home furnishing stores. A search of the Internet will doubtlessly yield many more products. Those listed below are similar to those we have been using for years.

*To adapt your bathtub faucet or shower to a gentle shower for baby swimming:*

**Water Saving Personal Shower—Handheld Shower Kit**
The kit includes a 59-inch white flexible hose, pushbutton shut-off control, and wall bracket. Connects to the shower arm. It can be found at: http://care2.greenhome.com/products/bath/bath_and_shower_filters/102031

## HOME SWIMMING ENVIRONMENTS

If you do not have a bathtub or your baby outgrows it, consider the environments below or search the Internet.

**Many Small Inexpensive Home Pools**
http://toys.about.com/od/sportsandoutdoorplay/tp/backyard pools.html

**More Small Inexpensive Home Pools**
www.inflateus.com/inflatablepools.htm

**How To Set Up or Convert to a Salt Water Pool**
www.poolplaza.com/C-Salt-Chlorinators.html

**AquaDoula**

This is a portable environment for water birthing. Also babies can swim in it. When babies grow out of it, it can be stored for the next baby. The circular environment is 54 inches in diameter and 25 inches deep. It can be found at http://www.aquadoula.com. Telephone number: 888-217-2229(BABY)

**Handmade Japanese Bath (Ofuro)**

I had my Japanese wooden bath shipped from Japan in the 1970s. Since those days, the dollar has fallen, and the yen has risen. I suspect the cost of buying and shipping a handmade bath must be exorbitant.

Searching the Internet using the key words "Japanese wood bath" or "Japanese wooden bath" will provide you with many options such as these:

SeaOtter Ofuros: Wooden ofuros
www.woodentubs.com/tubs_ofuro.html

Driftwood Handmade Wooden Baths
www.driftwood.ie/stan_ofuro.html

# Certificate of Achievement

## INDEPENDENT SWIMMER OF THE CRAWL STROKE

I do proudly certify that

on the _____ day of _____

my child

_____

at age _____

did entirely independently

dive into the water,

swim at least 12 yards or meters,

and climb out.

_____
Signed

# *About the Author*

**Douglas Doman** is the vice director of The Institutes for the Achievement of Human Potential. As president of The Institutes in Europe, he is responsible for The Institutes operations and families throughout Europe. He also serves on the board of directors of The Institutes in Mexico, where courses and the lecture series are presented annually.

As the son of Katie and Glenn Doman, he grew up on The Institutes campus with the brain-injured adults and children. He accompanied The Institutes research teams on three expeditions to study indigenous peoples while he was still in his early teens. In 1965 he studied the Navajo in Arizona; in 1967 he went to the Arctic to study the Inuits; and in 1969 he went to the Kalahari Desert, in Botswana, to live with and study the Bushmen. As part of his undergraduate study at Bard College, Douglas joined the Experiment in International Living. He studied child development among the Guambianos of Colombia, South America.

In 1975, at the invitation of the Sony Corporation, he went to Japan to teach English to tiny Japanese children. After living in Japan, Douglas went to Melbourne, Australia, to work with Tim and Claire Timmermans, world authorities in the techniques of teaching parents to teach their babies to swim.

Douglas's early years on the staff of The Institutes were spent creating the School for Human Development, a school for brain-injured young adults. He and his staff created the world's first

Human Development Course, a circuit utilizing physical activities that promote brain organization and development. They have made repeated breakthroughs in the field of children's physical development for both well babies and brain-injured children. The most important of these breakthroughs includes the quantification of children's physical development and working in collaboration with the National Aeronautics and Space Administration, Ames Research Center, on the design and creation of the Vehicle for Initial Crawling.

Douglas co-authored *How To Teach Your Baby To Be Physically Superb,* which has been translated into ten languages. It is an excellent companion book to this book.

He is married to Rosalind Klein Doman, associate director of The Institute for the Achievement of Physical Excellence. Their sons—Marlowe, Spencer, and Noah—and their daughter, Morgan, are the subjects of many of the photographs and discussions throughout this book.

# *Resources*

## QUESTIONS?

Write to:
Water Baby
The Institutes for the Achievement
   of Human Potential
8801 Stenton Avenue
Wyndmoor, PA 19038
Log in and ask at:
Website: http://waterbaby.iahp.org

## Courses for Parents

### *HOW TO MULITIPLY YOUR BABY'S INTELLIGENCE COURSE*

### *WHAT TO DO ABOUT YOUR BRAIN-INJURED CHILD COURSE*

*For information regarding these courses, please contact:*

The Institutes for the Achievement
   of Human Potential
8801 Stenton Avenue
Wyndmoor, PA 19038
Phone: 215-233-2050
Fax: 215-233-9646
Email: institutes@iahp.org
Website: www.iahp.org

## Books for Parents

### *HOW TO TEACH YOUR BABY TO BE PHYSICALLY SUPERB*

**Glenn Doman, Douglas Doman, and Bruce Hagy**

*How To Teach Your Baby To Be Physically Superb* explains the basic principles, philosophy, and stages of mobility in easy-to-understand language. This inspiring book describes just how easy and pleasurable it is to teach a young child to be physically superb. It clearly shows you how to create an environment for each stage of mobility that will help your baby advance and develop more easily. It shows that the team of mother, father, and baby is the most important athletic team your child will ever know. It explains how to begin, how to make your materials, and how to expand your program. This complete guide also includes full-color charts, photographs, illustrations, and detailed instructions to help you create your own program.

**Also available:**

*How To Teach Your Baby To Be Physically Superb Video or DVD*

## HOW SMART IS YOUR BABY?
### Develop and Nurture Your Newborn's Full Potential
**Glenn Doman and Janet Doman**

*How Smart Is Your Baby?* provides parents with all the information they need to help their baby achieve his or her full potential. The authors first explain the newborn's growth and development, including all of the critical stages involved. They then guide the parents in creating a home environment that enhances and enriches brain development. Most important, parents learn how to design an effective and balanced daily program for physical and intellectual growth. This joyous program brings parents and babies closer together, establishing a life-long bond of learning and love.

## HOW TO TEACH YOUR BABY TO READ
**Glenn Doman and Janet Doman**

*How To Teach Your Baby To Read* provides your child with the enjoyment of reading. It shows you just how easy and pleasurable it is to teach a young child to read. It explains how to begin and expand the reading program, how to make and organize your materials, and how to more fully develop your child's potential.

**Also available:**
*How To Teach Your Baby To Read Video or DVD*
*How To Teach Your Baby To Read Kits*

## HOW TO TEACH YOUR BABY MATH
**Glenn Doman and Janet Doman**

*How To Teach Your Baby Math* instructs you in successfully developing your child's ability to think and reason. It shows you just how easy and pleasurable it is to teach a young child math. It explains how to begin and expand the math program, how to make and organize your materials, and how to more fully develop your child's potential.

**Also available:**
*How To Teach Your Baby Math Video or DVD*
*How To Teach Your Baby Math Kits*

## HOW TO GIVE YOUR BABY ENCYCLOPEDIC KNOWLEDGE
**Glenn Doman, Janet Doman, and Susan Aisen**

*How To Give Your Baby Encyclopedic Knowledge* provides a program of visually stimulating information designed to help your child take advantage of his or her natural potential to learn anything. It shows you just how easy and pleasurable it is to teach a young child about the arts, science, and nature. Your child will recognize the insects in the garden, know the countries of the world, discover the beauty of a painting by van Gogh, and more. It explains how to begin and expand your program, how to make and organize your materials, and how to more fully develop your child's potential.

**Also available:**
*How To Give Your Baby Encyclopedic Knowledge Video*
*How To Give Your Baby Encyclopedic Knowledge Kits*

## HOW TO MULTIPLY YOUR BABY'S INTELLIGENCE
**Glenn Doman and Janet Doman**

*How To Multiply Your Baby's Intelligence* provides a comprehensive program that will enable your child to read, to do mathematics, and to learn about anything and everything. It shows you just how easy and pleasurable it is to teach your young child, and to help your child become more capable and confident. It explains how to begin and expand this remarkable program, how to make and organize your materials, and how to more fully develop your child's potential.

**Also available:**
*How To Multiply Your Baby's Intelligence Kits*

## WHAT TO DO ABOUT YOUR BRAIN-INJURED CHILD

### Glenn Doman

In this breakthrough book, Glenn Doman—pioneer in the treatment of the brain-injured—brings real hope to thousands of children, many of whom are inoperable, and many of whom have been given up for lost and sentenced to a life of institutional confinement. Based upon the decades of successful work performed at The Institutes for the Achievement of Human Potential, the book explains why old theories and techniques fail, and why The Institutes philosophy and revolutionary treatment succeed.

## IN FITNESS AND IN HEALTH

### Dr. Philip Maffetone

In *In Fitness and In Health—The No-Nonsense Guide to Diet, Exercise and Disease Prevention,* Dr. Maffetone describes a new approach to healthful living that will make you feel better, healthier, and fitter for the rest of your life by improving the choices you make and honing your natural instincts on diet and exercise.

## THE PATHWAY TO WELLNESS
**How To Help Your Brain-Injured Child or Your Brain-damaged, Mentally Retarded, Mentally Deficient, Cerebral Palsied, Epileptic, Autistic, Athetoid, Hyperactive, Attention Deficit Disordered, Developmentally Delayed, Down's Child**

### Glenn Doman and the Staff of The Institutes

This important book is written for parents whose children may have been given any of these labels and may have problems with movement, sensation, vision, hearing, language, learning, behavior, or a combination of these things. In addition, they may have problems with allergies, digestion, elimination, seizures, and general health and well-being, or may be in a coma. All of these are symptoms of brain injury. If your child has any of these symptoms or has been given any of these labels, this book is for you. It contains in simple terms what you need to know, what you should do, and what you should not do with your brain-injured child.

## TRAINING FOR ENDURANCE

### Dr. Philip Maffetone

In *Training For Endurance* Dr. Maffetone explains his MAF Program, his theories on stress and overtraining, instructions on warming up and cooling down, and other practical considerations for the endurance athlete. It includes complete training schedules for age-group athletes.

## Books for Children

Very young readers have special needs. These are not met by conventional children's literature, which is designed to be read by adults to little children, not by them. The careful choice of vocabulary, sentence structure, print size, and formatting is needed by very young readers. The design of these children's books is based upon a half-century of search and discovery of what works best for very young readers.

### *ENOUGH, INIGO, ENOUGH* (AGES 1 TO 6)
**written by Janet Doman**
**illustrated by Michael Armentrout**

### *NOSE IS NOT TOES* (AGES 1 TO 3)
**written by Glenn Doman**
**illustrated by Janet Doman**

## Bit of Intelligence Cards

### Anatomy
Organs of the Body

### Natural History

| | |
|---|---|
| Amphibians Set I | Insects Set II |
| Birds | Leaves |
| Birds of Prey | Mammals Set I |
| Butterflies and Moths | Mammals Set II |
| Dinosaurs | Primates Set I |
| Flowers Set I | Reptiles |
| Insects Set I | Sea Creatures |

### People

| | |
|---|---|
| Composers | Explorers |
| Great Inventors | |
| Presidents of the United States Set I | |
| World Leaders | |

### Mathematics
Regular Polygons

### Music
Musical Instruments

### Vehicles
Air Vehicles

### Works of Art
Great Art Masterpieces
Self-Portraits of Great Artists
Masterpieces by da Vinci
Masterpieces by Picasso
Masterpieces by van Gogh

## CD-ROMS

### *THE PICTURE DICTIONARY*

The Gentle Revolution Series includes ten volumes of the Picture Dictionary CD-ROMs.

The Picture Dictionary Program is designed to give parents a very easy-to-use method of introducing a program of encyclopedic knowledge in five different languages. A child may concentrate on a favorite language or gain ability in all five languages.

Each CD-ROM contains fifteen categories of Bit of Intelligence images, with ten images in each category. That is a total of 150 different images that can be viewed in English, Spanish, Japanese, Italian, and French on each CD-ROM.

For each image there is a large reading word provided. The child may choose to view the image and the reading word, the image alone, or the reading word alone. This program is so easy to navigate that children as young as three years old have been able to use it independently.

## WATERPROOF SWIMMING PROGRAM CHECKLISTS

*How To Teach Your Baby To Swim* contains seven checklists. Each checklist summarizes the contents of the chapter and a specific swimming program. These checklists have been made into convenient-size plastic cards and are attached to a comfortable wristband that parents can wear in the water. Parents can use the card to remember all the activities for each swimming session. A Water Safety and Hygiene checklist is included.

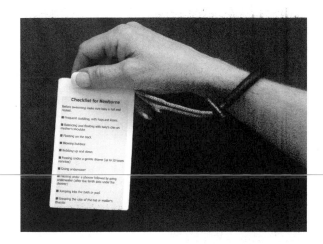

To purchase, call: 215-233-2050, ext. 2525 or toll-free 866-250-BABY.

## ASICS INFANT CRAWLING TRACK

The ASICS crawling track is constructed of yellow and green polyethylene foam and folds in half for portability and storage: 19" (49 cm) wide / 6.7" (17 cm) high / 46.5" (109 cm) long when opened.

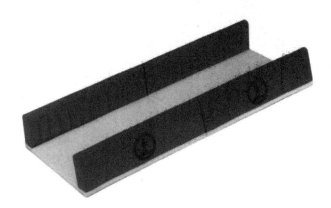

To purchase, call 215-233-2050, ext. 2525 or toll-free 866-250-BABY

*For information about these books and teaching materials, please contact:*

The Gentle Revolution Press
8801 Stenton Avenue
Wyndmoor, PA 19038
Phone: 215-233-2050, Ext. 2525
Fax: 215-233-3852
Toll-Free: 866-250-BABY
Email: info@gentlerevolution.com
www.gentlerevolution.com

# Index

Flutter kicks, 75, 80
Frequency of swims, 65–66
Genki, 25
Gessel, Arnold, 5
Goggles, 50–51
Grasp reflex, 27
*How Smart Is Your Baby?* (G. Doman, J.
 Doman), 7
*How To Give Your Baby Encyclopedic Knowledge*
 (G. Doman, D. Doman, Aisen), 68
*How To Multiply Your Baby's Intelligence* (G.
 Doman, J. Doman), 68
*How To Teach Your Baby To Be Physically Superb*
 (G. Doman, D. Doman, Hagy), 5
Hygiene, 50–52
Illnesses, water-related, 51
*In Fitness and In Health* (Maffetone), 90
Infants, teaching. *See* Newborns, teaching;
 Six- to twelve-month-olds, teaching.
Inhaling, 14–24, 37–41
Institutes for the Achievement of Human
 Potential, The, 1–2, 47, 65–66
Integrative areas, 68
Lake, swimming in a, 34
Maffetone, Philip, 90
Motor commands, 6–7
Newborns
 benefits of, swimming, 2
 teaching, 9–32
Ocean, swimming in an, 34
One- to two-year-olds, teaching, 53
Organization, importance of, 10, 44
Playtime, 83
Pool
 chemicals, 47–48
 climbing out of, 42–43, 59
 first time in the, 29, 33–34
 ideal depth of, for diving, 49
 toys, 83
 *See also* Hygiene; Safety.

Prehensile grasp, 28
Reflex, developmental, 27
Safety, 47–52
Senses, 6
Sensory stimulation, 6, 10
Shower, when to, 50
Siblings, 9, 49
Sisters. *See* Siblings.
Six- to twelve-month-olds, teaching, 33–45
Stimulation, 6
Streamlining, 76
Structure, importance of, 10, 44
Submerging, 22
Swimmer's itch, 51
Swimming
 benefits of learning, 2, 103
 competitively, 104
 on a full stomach, 11
 *See also* Teaching baby to swim.
Teaching baby to swim
 at four to six years old, 87–101
 at one to two years old, 53–66
 at six months old or younger, 9–32
 at six to twelve months old, 33–45
 at two to four years old, 67–86
Toddlers, teaching. *See* One- to two-year olds,
 teaching; Two- to four-year-olds,
 teaching.
Toys, 83
Two- to four-year-olds, teaching, 67–86
Vital release, 27
Water
 babies, 5
 -related illnesses, 51
 *See also* Hygiene; Safety.
Waterproof wristband, 117